9 Journeys Home

Other Books by Bob Mandel

Money Mantras
Open Heart Therapy
Two Hearts Are Better Than One
Heart Over Heels
Birth and Relationships (with Sondra Ray)
Wake Up to Wealth
Millennium Money Mantras (online publication)

9 Journeys Home

How to Get Back to Yourself

*Steps, Stops, Pitfalls, and Maps
to Guide You on Your Ultimate Adventure*

Bob Mandel

CELESTIAL ARTS
Berkeley | Toronto

Celestial Arts
P.O. Box 7123
Berkeley, California 94707
www.tenspeed.com

Distributed in Australia by Simon and Schuster Australia, in Canada by Ten Speed Press Canada, in New Zealand by Southern Publishers Group, in South Africa by Real Books, and in the United Kingdom and Europe by Airlift Book Company.

Cover design by Rebecca Neimark, Twenty-Six Letters
Text design by Chloe Nelson

Library of Congress Cataloging-in-Publication Data
Mandel, Robert Steven, 1943–
9 journeys home : how to get back to yourself : steps, stops, pitfalls, and maps to guide you on your ultimate adventure / Bob Mandel.
p. cm.
Includes index.
ISBN 1-58761-203-8
1. Self-actualization (Psychology). I. Title: Nine journeys home. II. Title.
BF575.S4M36   2003
158.1—dc21   2003009982

First printing, 2003
Printed in United States of America

1 2 3 4 5 6 7 8 9 10 — 07 06 05 04 03

This book is dedicated to my grandchildren—Ari, Sam, Jake, and Lily. God, how I love to play with you! God, how I am amazed by your differences, your uniqueness, your originality, your intelligence! You touch my heart so deeply. Watching you grow is the best show on earth, better than *The Lion King, The Little Mermaid, Toy Story, Shrek,* and *Star Wars* all rolled into one. You guys and gals are the best!

"Sometimes you have to go a long way out of your way
to find the shortest distance to where you're going."

—Edward Albee, *The Zoo Story*

"Life is a journey, not a guided tour."

—A hat I wear

Contents

Author's Note

There are many students and clients, adults and children, whose journeys contribute to this book, and I would like to acknowledge all of you. Indeed, I want to thank all those I've been blessed to work with since I began this work in 1976. You have taught me so much about love, healing, help, and support. Without you, this book would not exist, and, more importantly, I would not be the person I am today. To honor the sanctity of these relationships and the confidentiality of my work, I have changed all names, except those of my family members, who will have to endure my loving exposure of their insights and experiences. The quotes I use are gathered from my notes during and sometimes after sessions and seminars, and therefore may not always be 100 percent accurate, but I believe I have represented each person quite faithfully and apologize if and when I have not.

These journeys represent the major lessons of the International Self-Esteem Project, which I founded in 1998 and have since been sharing in schools and seminars around the world. Each journey is composed of many steps and stories. Some tell the tales of my own soul; some recount stories from my wife, Mallie; my children; my grandchildren; as well as clients and children I have encountered in various classrooms. All these stories are honest and humble examples of journeys home. I believe that each of us is on a path to home, a path that sometimes seems solitary but inevitably entails relationship. I present these nine directions as adventures in internal landscape, using the metaphor of external trails to describe inner states of being. It is both my prayer and my intention that these journeys help you find your way and provide some excitement on the back roads of your mind.

Acknowledgments

I would like to acknowledge so many people whose work, research, teachings, and support have influenced me in writing this book. First of all, Mallie, besides being my muse and best fan, has been a great first reader and editor of all my books, especially this one. She is the one who notices all the little details while always keeping sight of the big picture. I also want to thank Dr. Thomas Verny for his pioneering work in pre- and perinatal psychology as well as his friendship, support, and feedback on the first draft. I also thank Dr. David Chamberlain for his inspiration and warmth. Dr. Stephen Wolinsky's work on quantum psychology, chaos, false identities, the inner child, and enneagrams has affected me deeply, helping to cause a shift in my awareness at a very important transition in my life. Caroline Myss's book *Anatomy of the Spirit,* plus her talks on healing, "woundology," and closure, have also had a profound effect on my outlook. The research and exciting presentations of Dr. Bruce Lipton in the areas of cellular biology and DNA development have had a major impact on my thinking, as has the genius and passion of Joseph Chilton Pierce. Thomas Armstrong, author of *7 Kinds of Smart,* whose popularization of the concept of multiple intelligences opened many windows in my mind, has been a great support without even knowing it. I also want to express gratitude and appreciation to Dr. Deepak Chopra for his revolutionary view of the human body, Dr. Michel Odent for his talk on "the future of a civilization born under anesthesia," and Dr. Larry Dossey for his research on the power of prayer, the soul, and the mind. Much thanks also to Barbara Findeisen and her kind words of support for the International Self-Esteem Project. I am also grateful for the role that *A Course in Miracles* continues to play in my spiritual life. Thank you to APPPAH, the Association for Pre- and Perinatal Psychology and Health, for all your good work and your love of children.

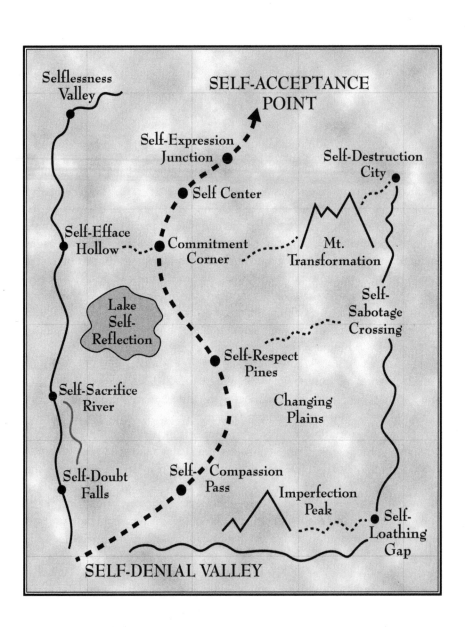

Journey 1

The Road to Self-Acceptance

The road to self-acceptance is a journey *from* you *to* you. You move out of self-denial through self-compassion into self-respect and on to self-expression. On this first road you discover your commitment to yourself and learn how to stand up for yourself when necessary. You also find the motivation to make important changes. When you reach the point of self-acceptance, you've arrived at the turning point of your life.

You are who you are and you will always be that person. You may grow, improve, transform, and develop certain aspects of yourself, but you are the one doing all that growing. You are who you are, not what you do, what you feel, or what you think. You are the container of all your experience, and the space in which it all happens. Accepting yourself is saying yes to that space, validating what it contains. It's okay to be you, having the experience you're having. Of course, you are not always happy; you want to change some things, maybe many things; and life is far from perfect. You strive to be a better person, to overcome your deficiencies and develop healthier habits. Nevertheless, you are who you are. When you're angry, you're angry. When you feel hurt, you feel hurt. And when you're happy, you're happy. It's okay to be you, a feeling person. Perhaps you eat too much, drink too much, smoke cigarettes, talk behind people's backs, tell lies, scream at your kids, or tailgate. Okay, you're not a perfect human being. You've got a problem. Nevertheless, you are the one and only you, and you are the one who can do something about it. Accept yourself. It's your life. It all begins and ends with you.

❖ ❖ ❖ ❖ ❖ ❖ ❖ ❖ ❖ ❖

Carlos came to me like a breath of fresh air. He was a participant in an advanced intensive training program I conduct every summer near my home in the hills of northwestern Connecticut. On the surface, he was a winner— handsome, successful, happily married with two children. He could light up a room with the flash of his smile, always had a good joke up his sleeve, and offered a shoulder to lean on for all takers.

Trouble was, Carlos couldn't accept himself. In his mind, he had never been good enough for his father, who died some years back, and therefore he felt like a disappointment to anyone who loved him. It was quite a trap. The more you loved him, the more his self-esteem plummeted and the more he became convinced that you didn't really know him. Moreover, whenever he was happy, which was often, he didn't believe he deserved to feel so good. His solution was to bottle himself up. When he introduced himself each day, he'd say he felt "so-so," "fine," or "okay," hiding his overwhelming feelings of happiness, not wanting to make anyone else feel bad. Putting joy in a bottle was hard work for Carlos.

Like many of us, Carlos seemed to have two sides—the shining armor of his public persona and the dark shadow he feared and hid from the world. Half my work with him was to help him to see that his magnificence was real, and that when he hid it from others the world was a darker place. The other half was making it okay not to be perfect. In other words, Carlos needed to accept what was so.

I began by encouraging him to accept his happiness as something he deserved to feel. We worked on stretching his "acknowledgment ceiling"— allowing himself to receive more love from others than he had from his father. When he replied that the more others loved him, the more he felt obligated to them, I urged him to see the situation in a new light—perhaps the joy of loving him was reward enough, and perhaps his resistance to receiving was hurtful toward others. He said he'd have to sleep on that one.

The next day I supported him in sharing himself fully and freely with the group. When he responded that he had nothing important to share, I reminded him that *he* was important and therefore everything he felt was important. I also mentioned that he did not have to have a big problem to be worthy of sharing. His happiness was equally important to someone else's misery. "You mean, I don't have to pretend to be manic-depressive in order to belong?" he joked. I found myself cheering for Carlos with all my heart.

His role model was Phil Jackson, the celebrity Zen/basketball coach. Carlos admired the man's ability to maintain his calm in all circumstances. The image of the coach quietly cleaning his eyeglasses with ten seconds remaining in a tied game was especially strong for Carlos. When I suggested that Michael Jordan might be a better role model for him, he asked why. I told him Jackson was too cool and aloof while Jordan was both hot and hungry—intense, passionate, and involved. I added that it was okay to be emotional, to blow it once in a while, to be human.

"You mean, I should forgive myself for not being perfect? What a concept!"

During the ten days of the workshop, Carlos opened up and began to accept himself more and more. The group teased him about being a mess, a screw-up, and a flop. His was a journey from trying to be perfect to accepting his imperfection. A director of TV soap operas and dramas, he confessed that while waiting for the Venezuelan TV awards to be announced he hated himself for how competitive he felt. I recommended that he visualize his father presenting him with an award for being good enough as a son. He smiled. The next day he came in with a new book he had bought, *The Spirituality of Imperfection.* "Great title," I commented.

As our time together was drawing to a close, Carlos shared his fear of going home. Tears squirted from his eyes. "It's been like a womb here. I am afraid that when I go back to reality, I'll leave all these wonderful feelings behind." Somehow, I doubted it. The last day we were all in the pool doing a process I call "new baptism." We stood in a circle and one by one each person took his place in the center, declaring a new belief about himself, whereupon he submerged himself in the water as we all cheered. When it was his turn, Carlos took his place at the center, flashed his winning smile, and shouted, "I baptize myself in the thought that from now on I am my own role model!" Go, Carlos!

◇ ◇ ◇ ◇

You have the right to be you. This is your birthright, the most fundamental of all human rights—the right to develop a healthy sense of self. But do you *want* to be you? What good is a human right if you don't exercise your claim to it? In the case of self-esteem, the road to self-acceptance is the first journey toward self-love and self-actualization. When I mention this to people, often they don't get it. They think that self-criticism leads to self-improvement and that self-acceptance generates complacency. They believe the old myth that disapproving, judging, and punishing themselves will build character and make themselves better people.

Imagine that there is an internal courtroom residing in your mind. You are constantly on trial. There is not even a jury. Only a judge, a prosecuting attorney, and a defense attorney. The attorneys make their cases, call their witnesses, argue back and forth. As you watch these people go through the motions of justice, you realize they are all you. You are the actor playing all these parts. And what is the trial about? You are on trial for your life because you have killed someone. Yourself. Suddenly, you, the *real* you, storm into the courtroom and proclaim, "What are all you people doing in *my* mind! I'm alive, not dead! You all get out of here this instant! This court is adjourned!"

THE ROAD TO SELF-ACCEPTANCE

Get out of the courtroom and embark on the road to Self-Acceptance Point. Move out of Self-Denial Valley and head for Self-Compassion Pass, where you can find the same empathy for yourself that you normally reserve for others. Ask for directions if necessary, but don't miss Self-Respect Pines, where your self-esteem finds dignity and leads you to Commitment Corner, where you notice what's out of integrity in your life and commit yourself to being all you can be. Eventually, you will reach your Self Center and find your way to Self-Expression Junction, which lies just below Self-Acceptance Point. Knowing that you are important, and that what you say is valuable, you will learn to stand up for yourself and tell the world how you feel. Having finally arrived at Self-Acceptance Point, you can say yes to yourself.

One of the saddest things is when a child hates herself. Lisa was seven and, according to her single mother, seemed to have a self-esteem problem. She would wake up in the middle of the night screaming, "I hate myself! I hate my life!" When I asked her why she thought she said these things, she said it was because all the other kids made fun of her.

"So, it's them you hate, not yourself."

"No," she cried, "I like everyone. It's just me I can't stand."

"I'm sorry the kids are so cruel to you."

"Why do they have to pick on me all the time?"

"Maybe it's because they're jealous?"

"Jealous of what?"

"Well, for one thing, you're very pretty and very smart."

"That's two things."

"You see. I told you you were smart." She smiled. I knew I could make her feel better, but I worried whether she could make herself feel better. After a while, she said, "I just wish I was dead sometimes." When I asked her why, she replied that she didn't really know, she just had that feeling. I told her I would miss her very much if she were dead, and so would a lot of other people, even the kids who were teasing her.

At the end of our time together, I suggested that Lisa give herself a big hug and pretend she was her own big sister. She did what I asked, rocking herself and saying, "It's okay, sis. You're going to be just fine."

Compassion for oneself can seem self-indulgent, but I believe it's a healthy choice. Most people are fairly compassionate toward others, but when it comes to themselves they fail miserably. You deserve your own compassion. When you are having a hard time, give yourself a break. Talk to yourself. Embrace yourself. Give yourself a shoulder to lean on. Sometimes I look in the mirror and say, "I'm sorry you're having such a rough day." Usually, the guy looking back at me smiles. He appreciates me.

◇ ◇ ◇ ◇

Some exciting new research in the area of birth and psychology—in particular the work of Dr. Thomas Verny and Dr. Bruce Lipton—has suggested that children are learning, growing, decision-making beings even when they are in the womb. Thus, if a child is wanted for "the wrong reason"—for example, conceived to save a marriage, replace a miscarried child, or fill up some other emptiness in the parents—he may have a problem accepting himself. He might even "inherit" the emptiness of the mother that he felt in the womb, feeling that he can never be good enough to fulfill anyone, including himself.

I mention this not to make mothers guilty or hyper-conscious of their every emotion but rather so that they might be more aware of this dynamic and thus able to offer their children the reassurance they need in case they got off to a difficult start in life. We want to support our children in knowing that they are wanted, welcome, and good enough for themselves as well as the ones they love.

Lisa's mother found herself pregnant as a teenager. She was unmarried but in love with a street kid. Lisa's conception was an act of rebellion against her mom's disapproving parents. Throughout the pregnancy, the thought of abortion was in the air. It is possible that the mere thought of abortion during pregnancy might contribute to the depression of a child, even to thoughts of suicide. In fact, there could very well be a direct link between teenage suicide and babies who are not entirely wanted. It seems that the combination of maternal rejection and birth complications tends to contribute to an increase in teenagers' violence toward themselves and others. It's as though the mother's lack of certainty about having the child causes the child to be uncertain about herself in many ways.

Lisa had some cards stacked against her. But she was surrounded by a very loving extended family, and I felt confident that, given time, she would come not only to like herself, but to enjoy her life as well. Not all unwanted children are as fortunate as Lisa.

I was visiting my granddaughter Ariana's class. There were twenty-two nine-year-olds listening to me talk about self-esteem. I mentioned that I heard they had a game in their school called "caught being good." If a child did something good—such as help an old lady across the street, pick up a book if someone dropped it, or hold a door open for a teacher—and another student reported it, then the child was called to the principal's office. The principal called the parents, who were told that their child was caught being good. The local newspaper was also notified. The child received a reward, had his picture taken and published in the newspaper, and became a sort of local hero.

I asked the children how they liked this game. They replied that it was great. When I asked why, they said they liked getting all the approval, attention, and rewards. Then I asked them the following questions. "How would you feel if you did something really good and nobody noticed you or reported you?" There was a long silence. Ariana raised her hand and I nodded. "I would feel just as good," she said, "because I would know that I did something really good." I smiled, knowing that she was well on her way to a healthy sense of self.

SELF-RESPECT PINES

Imagine entering the mountain village of Self-Respect Pines. There is something in the air and altitude that affects everyone with self-respect. You can see it in the faces of people walking down Main Street. Even the young children have a sweet sense of dignity. You take a deep breath and you are filled with a feeling of self-respect, happy to be who you are. You pull your car over by a huge pine tree. You look at yourself in the rearview mirror and say, "Yes, yes, yes. I respect you."

It is terribly tempting to praise and reward our children when they attain or accomplish something important. However, it is far more valuable in the long run if you ask your child how he or she feels about the accomplishment before you bestow your praises. A child who is able to validate himself is developing an internal knowing that will last a lifetime. While praise surely beats disapproval, it is no substitute for the ability to accept and validate oneself.

When I ask children why self-esteem is so important, most reply that it helps you to be more successful in life. A few, however, tell me that self-esteem is important because with it, when things are hard, you can still know you are a good person. How wise a child can be. When you fail at something and your self-esteem is low, the experience is devastating and you can wallow in self-loathing for ages. By contrast, when you are struggling and yet remember your self-esteem, doing so enables you to recover more quickly and, in addition, helps you not take your problems too personally.

You can accept yourself, acknowledge your problems, and look for solutions.

Accepting yourself does not mean you don't want to improve. Your right to be you is based, in part, on the natural desire you have to improve yourself and realize your full potential. You have an inherent inclination to express your unlimited self. Go for it! And when you stumble on the path, then it's time to look at what you've stumbled on, because it is clearly a gift, or a lesson to be explored. You need to learn from your lessons, your karma, the feedback the universe is generously reflecting back to you. When you don't learn your lesson the first time, the universe kindly affords you another opportunity.

What you have difficulty accepting about yourself usually falls into two categories. The first is what you have not forgiven in yourself. The second is what you need to change. Some things, such as being more intelligent, beautiful, or talented than another, just need self-forgiveness. In fact, these qualities are not problems; they are gifts. The only problem is your guilt that holds you back. So forgive yourself for your greatness and get going.

Other things . . . well, perhaps they require a little self-improvement. It's not enough simply to forgive yourself for slandering others, taking what's not yours, or striking out violently at someone. You need to make amends. It's humbling to admit that you need to apologize to another human being, but sometimes saying "I'm sorry" is the most pragmatic and spiritually wise decision you can make. Of course, at the same time you want to forgive yourself for your poor behavior. The combination of forgiving yourself and apologizing to another returns you to a state of guiltlessness and grace.

All the great religions teach us self-acceptance. "Love thy neighbor as thyself" is grounded in the premise of self-love. Abraham, Jesus, Mohammed, Buddha—none of them ever said, "Love your neighbor, hate yourself."

Chastity was a client of mine from the '80s who, after many years away from counseling, came back for help with a specific problem. She had written a play about her father, but her playwriting teacher claimed he owned half the rights. Having been abused by her father, she was repeating the pattern with the teacher, who vowed to do anything within his power—which was considerable—to block the play's production. As I interviewed Chastity, it became apparent that she was blaming herself in part for having allowed the teacher's name to appear alongside hers at an early staging of the play. As with many abused children, she was looking for the reasons she was creating such unfair treatment. Finally, I said to her point blank, "Maybe you just have to learn to stand up for yourself!" I supported her in standing up to this professional abuse, finding a good lawyer, summoning all her resources, and feeling her power. I suggested that perhaps this lesson was even more important than the fate of her play. She took my advice and began gathering evidence from other students as she mounted her crusade against her abusive teacher. A few months later she sent me an email reporting that she had won her case and that her teacher had relinquished all claim to her creation.

Standing up for yourself is an important sign on the road to self-acceptance. Knowing that you deserve standing up for is a major step on the journey. Learning how to forgive the one who attacks you at the same time that you stand tall shows the true meaning of "turning the other cheek"—not that you should resign yourself to more abuse, but rather that you should let your abuser know how ineffective his behavior is.

So please, stand up for yourself as you are, with both your blessings and your problems. Accept the wonder of your essential self—the you beyond all appearances. There is no reward for self-rejection. The punishment you inflict on yourself is pain without gain. I know you want to achieve more in your life. I know you want to feel spiritually whole as well. You can attain your golden vision without attacking yourself for your slipups. You are well on your way. Stop, smell the roses, and acknowledge yourself. You have come far. Enjoy the journey. The future is unknown but there is nothing to fear.

Accept who you are.

Avoid comparisons.

You're the one and only you.

SELF-EXPRESSION JUNCTION

Stand up and strut around the room. Point your thumb at your chest. Repeat ten times to yourself, "I'm the one and only me!" Now rise up on your toes and proclaim, "I'm important!" Repeat it over and over. Go sit in front of a mirror, point at yourself with conviction, and affirm, "You are a VIP!" Repeat ten times. Open the window and declare to your neighborhood, "I'm the most important person in my life." It's okay if you turn a few heads. After all, you've entered Self-Expression Junction.

Carlos returned to me one year later. The first day, he shared along with everyone else. His smile once again lit up the room, but his words were somber. He told the story of coming to my workshop a year ago, wanting to be like Phil Jackson, the cool basketball coach, Mr. Perfect. He recounted how he learned to accept his own imperfections, even laugh at them. But when he went home, the proverbial excrement really hit the fan. He resumed his work directing a soap opera and found he had no patience with all the incompetent people surrounding him. People would ask stupid questions and he would snap at them. Others were lazy and would want him to do their jobs. He would blow up in their faces. In the end he felt more like Bobby Knight, the hot-tempered, chair-throwing coach, than the Zen-like Phil Jackson. He couldn't understand what had happened to him.

He was willing to accept his imperfection. But his inhumanity?

In the course of the program, Carlos unraveled the real reasons he could not compete with Phil Jackson for the title of Mr. Cool.

Carlos shared that he had been strongly attracted to a beautiful actress whom he was directing in the soap opera. She was attracted to him as well. He never told his wife, and therefore felt trapped between his attraction and

9

his secrecy. Although he never followed through on his attraction, his guilt was enormous. The tension at work became unbearable, causing him to lash out at people.

Carlos went deeper, returning to a scene when he was twelve years old. His mother had taken him on a vacation with her lover. The boy was devastated but he could not say anything to either his mother or his father. He became the keeper of the family secret. The emotion of the twelve-year-old was alive and well in Carlos the grown-up. The soap opera of his childhood had erupted on the actual set of his adult life.

Understanding his past, Carlos was able to forgive himself for his conflicting emotions and accept this state of confusion. Then he went home and made peace with his wife.

◇ ◇ ◇ ◇

Accepting yourself is embracing yourself with all your confusion, complications, and complexity. The simple act of acceptance dissolves all resistance. I remember when I was a child we had this toy called Chinese handcuffs. You stuck one finger from each hand into a flexible paper tube. When you pulled your fingers the hole got tighter and you couldn't get free. The only way out was to relax into the opening. So it is with yourself. What you resist persists. When you surrender, you release.

Take the necessary steps on the road to Self-Acceptance Point. Without them, you stay stuck on the back roads of self-denial, self-doubt, and self-loathing, wandering in the foothills of your full potential. Even in the hills of hopelessness, however, all is not lost. Acceptance still beckons you. When you simply accept the fact that you are trapped in self-rejection, you begin to loosen the Chinese handcuffs once more. Acceptance can happen at any moment, at any juncture. Whenever it happens, your life turns around completely. Like a train entering a roundhouse, you enter heading one way and leave moving in an entirely new direction. Acceptance thereby corrects your development midjourney.

Self-acceptance is the womb from which self-esteem is born.

The Pitfall

The *pitfall* on the journey of self-acceptance is resignation. If you mistakenly believe that accepting yourself implies that your lot in life will never change, improve, or transform, you are misunderstanding the context for self-acceptance. To accept yourself is to respect and have compassion for the being that you are. This does not mean that you are no longer self-critical. On the contrary, it is because you honor who you are that you can evaluate your life in the light of your highest vision for yourself. In other words, you assess what it is about your life that is incongruent with your essential self. Then you commit yourself to changing your behavior, not because you think you are worthless and insignificant, but, on the contrary, because you respect yourself and know you are not living up to your true nature. For example, if you are smoking, drinking, or otherwise neglecting your body, instead of condemning yourself and descending into self-loathing, you wake up one day and say to yourself, "I love myself too much to abuse my body in this way." From this realization, you commit yourself to change. You might want to create an *integrity checklist*. Write down the major categories of your life that need attention: your body, communication with others, money, your house, and so on. Review the list periodically and see which categories you feel out of integrity with, and consider what steps you need to take to get back into integrity. Keep in mind that being in integrity with yourself is what matters the most. You can use this list to support yourself. Be careful, though, that you don't use it to beat up yourself. You can have a system for self-correction based on self-love. You know that self-loathing and self-pity never motivated anyone to improve. But love—including self-love—can move mountains, or at least make their peaks more accessible.

Steps on the First Journey

1. Say yes to yourself.
2. Develop compassion for yourself.
3. Respect yourself.
4. Remember that nobody is perfect.
5. Forgive yourself.
6. Commit yourself to self-improvement.
7. Change your behavior when appropriate.
8. Center yourself.
9. Express yourself.
10. Stand up for yourself when necessary.
11. Know that you're important.

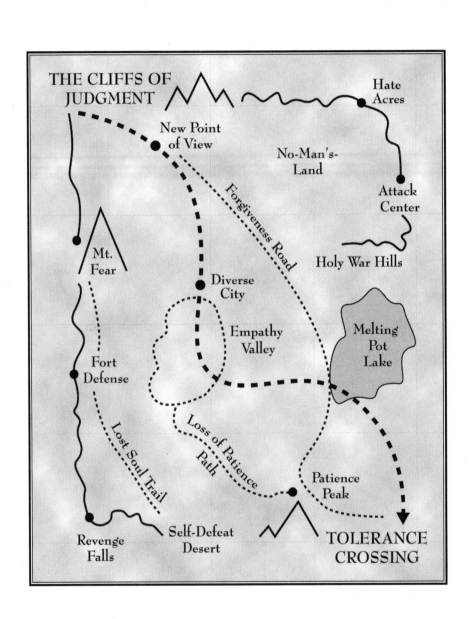

Journey 2

The Trail of Tolerance

The journey from self-acceptance to self-actualization can seem like a long and lonely one, but in fact it always involves relationships. A friend of mine tells the story of going to India to be with his guru at an ashram. Every day he meditated, prayed, worshipped, chanted, sat in a cave, and bathed himself in the holy river. After six years his guru sent him away, telling him he had learned everything. He returned to the States certain he was enlightened, a permanent peace embracing his consciousness. One day he went home to visit his parents and his mother made a sarcastic comment. Suddenly he found himself screaming at her with more wrath than he thought humanly possible.

The journey home ultimately leads you down the trail of tolerance. Relationships cannot be avoided. Self-acceptance must be extended to include others for it to be integrated. To accept yourself in a vacuum is to confine yourself to isolation. To become tolerant of those who are different from you is to embrace the unknown parts of your own psyche as well as the diversity of the world.

We tend to judge what we fear or do not understand. Tolerance is therefore the road to accepting our own fears and limitations. It also takes us through the valley of empathy and leads us to open-mindedness.

When I become tolerant of someone who sees things differently, I am admitting that I don't know it all, that I may be wrong from time to time, and that love is more important than right or wrong. I would rather win love than wars.

Of course, there are many things I cannot tolerate. I find violence and cruelty to be intolerable. I see a parent abusing a child and I want to run to rescue the innocent victim. Nevertheless, who am I to judge? And even when I cannot help it, I must remind myself that I am judging a behavior, not a fellow human being.

When I embrace tolerance, I embrace myself, even with my flaws.

◇ ◇ ◇ ◇ ◇ ◇ ◇ ◇ ◇ ◇

Irene stormed through the house like a hurricane bent on severe damage. She swaggered as though she were a monsoon about to wreak havoc. And she vented her emotions like a mighty river inundating all in her path.

Sometimes the journey home encounters inclement weather.

Irene had a gift, but it was well wrapped. Her personality seemed formed with the sole intention of keeping people at a distance, and she was quite successful at it. Her lack of boundaries was notorious in my group. Within a few weeks, she informed all of us that her mother never taught her any boundaries, which seemed to be a blatant excuse to have none.

Irene knew how to throw her considerable weight around, and often did. She would push you out of the way and make a mad dash to the most comfortable chair in the house. Unfortunately, the house was mine and the chair as well, a beautiful soft, blue chaise longue, and one day Irene actually walked across it as though it were a rug on her way to the bathroom—or refrigerator; I can't remember which. What I do recall is the sound of the poor springs as she sent the innards into permanent disarray. I am sure the chair is still working on forgiving her.

You can tell by now that I have a special place in my heart for Irene.

She was a walking, talking lesson in tolerance. Every time she moved or opened her mouth, you would have the opportunity to condemn or accept her. In the course of a nine-month intensive training program, there was no avoiding her. She was the oldest sibling and daddy's favorite, but she always had to take care of the others. Now it was her turn.

In time most of the group looked at Irene from a new point of view, and as they did she revealed another side of herself. She was naïve, vulnerable, and curious about everything. She wanted to know why her life was the way it was, what thoughts were creating what results, and what patterns she needed to unravel to lose weight, be happier in her marriage, become more successful in life. We came to see that Irene had an enormous appetite for life (as well as food), and that her need for nourishment was a common denominator for everyone. Moreover, she had a wonderful sense of humor and a warm heart.

Nothing was getting in the way of Irene's journey home. Her commitment to her goal was like a force of nature. Irene was a tour guide on the Trail of Tolerance. She showed us the way down from the Cliffs of Judgment to Forgiveness Road. She led us to Empathy Valley and pointed out Patience Peak. If we wandered off on Loss of Patience Path, she steered us back to Diverse City or Melting Pot Lake. Eventually, we all arrived at Tolerance Crossing. Thank you, Irene.

When you learn to accept yourself, it is easier to be tolerant of others. But it can also work the other way around. Sometimes, learning to be tolerant of others opens the door to greater self-acceptance. Whichever way you go, one of the most valuable keys to happiness and success in life is tolerance.

Usually we think of tolerance as a quality to be practiced toward strangers, and I will address that aspect further on. But tolerance, like most spiritual qualities, begins at home. It is no accident that most violence in the world is domestic in nature. It is the people you live closest to who bring up the fiercest reactions. They can be mates, parents, children, siblings, or even the infamous in-laws. Inhabiting a single dwelling with other relatives, especially but not necessarily when space is limited, can bring up strong primal, territorial emotions. So, while it is true that we should treat strangers as kindly as our own families, it is not always true that we treat our families so kindly.

We tend to be intolerant when we feel threatened. While it is often obvious in international disputes why one group of people might feel threatened by another, relationships at home can be more subtle. The bottom line is, people tend to feel threatened by things they don't understand, things that are different, or things that touch hidden truths in themselves that they fear facing. When your self-esteem is high, you generally feel less threatened by differences. But if you are insecure about your own identity, being in contact with someone whose sense of self seems strong yet quite different from yours can elicit fear, anger, judgment, even condemnation.

DIVERSE CITY

You're walking downtown in Diverse City. The streets are crowded with all types of people. Tall, short, fast, slow, with different colored skins, language, hair, dress, and demeanor. As you walk on, you relax more and more, feeling your acceptance of the diversity that surrounds you. In the middle of the city is a wooded area, and it is deserted. You are drawn to the sound of drums in the woods. It is late and dark, but you feel safe. As you enter the woods, you see a fire burning. You approach where the drum and fire are and you notice a circle of people standing around the fire. The circle includes all the important people from your life— mother, father, grandparents, siblings, friends, lovers, teachers, and people for whom you have had special antagonism as well. You take your place in the circle. One by one, each person dances to the drumbeat, doing the unique dance of his or her soul around the fire. As each person dances, you can love each one, celebrating the diversity of every individual. Now, it is your turn to dance. See yourself dance. When the dance is over, everyone stands together, holding hands in the circle. Then you walk in your separate directions back to your lives.

In a marriage, two people need to reconcile their differences if they are to experience a happy union. All marriages can be said to be mixed, in a sense. First of all, they are mixed sexually, assuming opposite-sex marriage. They can also be mixed religiously, philosophically, or psychologically. Partners can disagree about politics, people, and places, each having a strong but opposite position. I have seen couples turn ugly toward each other while discussing a president, a movie, or what color car they should purchase.

In my marriage, we are very different. I was born Jewish, Mallie was born Protestant. I'm from a big city, she's from a small town. I'm tall, she's short. I tend to be in a hurry, she tends to slow down. Or, as you can see from the way I have written this paragraph, I have a need to go first while she is more likely to follow. We attribute the fast/slow thing to our "birth scripts," since I was born fast but had to wait afterward before connecting with my mom, while Mallie's mom felt like it was taking forever when she came out. When we first got together, we struggled with the *dyadic dance.* Should the dance be slow or fast, or can one partner dance fast and the other slow and still achieve the goal of the dance—which is to be together? I remember that we'd be going to lead some seminars in Europe, the bags would be packed, and I'd feel my heart pumping as I loaded the car. It would be hours before we needed to be at the airport, but I'd be rushing anyway. Mallie meanwhile would be carefully checking the house, taking care of details, making sure we hadn't forgotten anything, that all the lights were off, and so on. The longer she took the more I would rush her, and the more I would rush her the longer she took. Sound familiar?

As we became more tolerant of each other's rhythms, some interesting things happened. First, each of us began to laugh at his or her own pace. We could see the absurdity of the dance. Secondly, I began to slow down and Mallie began to speed up. It seemed as though the less I pressured her, the faster she moved. Also, the less I pressured her, the less I pressured myself. I began to feel that "slowly was holy," and I appreciated all the details Mallie was handling at the perfectly appropriate pace. I also found that while she was going slow, I had a choice. I did not have to feel as if I was waiting. I could use that extra time to do something, such as read, write, or meditate. Finally, I realized that I had this enormous judgment about fast and slow, thinking that faster was better. After all, if you went fast, you could cross the finish line first. What finish line? I began to feel the futility underneath all my rushing and racing and made it a major goal for myself to slow down, stay in the present time, and feel that time was on my side, to quote an old song. I learned patience, which is an important ingredient in tolerance. Taking my time seemed to create more time, while racing against time always felt like a losing proposition. Practicing patience was a great lesson in tolerance for me.

Ironically, in the end I came to see how rapidly Mallie accomplished many tasks and how slow I was in many areas of my life. Eventually, the entire issue of fast and slow, versus slow and fast, seemed to dissolve from our relationship, although it can still pop up in humorous ways during times of stress.

Another important aspect of tolerance is respect. As you raise your awareness of self, you come to respect yourself and others. We all deserve equal respect. No matter where a person is from, what she looks like, how old or young she is, how rich or poor—she deserves your respect. In a family, respecting the differences can be the foundation for healthy relationships. When a child loses respect for a parent, her whole world caves in. Of course, it can be natural for a child to go through a phase where she no longer sees her parents as gods and realizes they are just human beings. Such a realization is healthy, but when it is accompanied by loss of respect it is devastating. When a teenager, for example, thinks his parents are too old to know anything, his intolerance sets him back. In any tribe, or family, as children grow they need to learn from *the wisdom of the elders.* When they lose sight of this wisdom, they become blind to their place in the circle of life.

Adults must also learn to have great patience, respect, and tolerance for their children. Parents may have an understandable inclination to think that their children, being young and inexperienced, are somehow less intelligent than they are. Secretly, they may fear their children know more than they do because, after all, every parent knows he doesn't know it all. The truth is, a child's intelligence is in place from birth, indeed before, and by age three his brain is performing at peak potential. A parent therefore needs to learn to listen to what his child is thinking, feeling, and expressing because, when the bridge of communication collapses, the family is fractured and the child is alienated from the love, attention, and support he needs. An enlightened parent will respect her child, hear what is being said, not putting words in the child's mouth or evaluating the spoken words. Teaching the child to validate himself, this type of parent will not fall into approval or disapproval modes but, rather, will ask the child how he feels about what he is sharing.

When children respect *the wisdom of the elders* and parents respect *the natural knowing of the children,* a mutual understanding develops and a nonjudgmental forum is created that leads to greater tolerance in the family. Remember, even in the best of families there can be a healthy difference of opinion. When each member of the family learns that it is okay to think for himself and it is also okay for others to disagree, that family is a secure and loving one whose members can come and go.

To be tolerant, one must sometimes endure difficult things. But one should never be tolerant of abuse. It is one thing to know that whatever you are attracted to in this life has some important lesson for you, and that there are no accidents. This attitude helps you turn every situation into a win, developing your sense of self in each moment by accepting, unraveling, and understanding what you are going through. But when you are faced with someone who is violently abusing you, it would be a serious mistake to stay in that situation and justify it by thinking you attracted it to grow and learn. Being tolerant of the failures of others is an important aspect of love and compassion. Being tolerant of what is clearly destructive to you, however, is a sign of low self-esteem and of terrible confusion about what you are responsible for in your life. So, when you are confronted by abusive situations, the healthy choice is to remove yourself from the scene and then, afterward, you can figure out why (or if) you were attracted to it.

✧ ✧ ✧

Miranda is the daughter of former clients and current friends of mine. When she was sixteen, she was going through a difficult period in her life. The family had moved from Brooklyn to a small, snobbish town in Connecticut, and Miranda had strong feelings of not belonging. She was Jewish, to begin with, and while anti-Semitism was not rampant in the community, it may have been in the air. Certainly, her peers were very exclusive, which she abhorred, leaving her to feel judged, criticized, and condemned by many of them. Moreover, she was having a hard time with her father, who she felt was using her for "target practice." It did not help that her mother was smothering her with worry and concern. To make matters worse, both her parents were schoolteachers who associated self-esteem with academic performance. Physically, Miranda was suffering from a form of epilepsy that was frightening, exhausting, and troublesome to the whole family.

Miranda was afraid she might have a seizure during her session, but I assured her she could relax and breathe through whatever came up. Some clients talk very little when they do a session of breathwork. Others, especially the nervous ones, chatter. Miranda started chattering. She was complaining about how the kids at school treated her, how her parents treated her, and how she felt completely persecuted in her life. Finally, she said, "I feel like I'm in a concentration camp," at which point her body began to shake uncontrollably. She said she thought she might be beginning a seizure. I asked her if she was afraid and she replied no. I supported her physically and verbally and she did fine. She began to talk about her relatives who had been in concentration camps. She wondered if she had been in one in a past life. She asked me if I thought she could have been gassed and was reexperiencing those sensations in her seizures. I said nothing but let her go where she needed to go. Finally, toward the end of the session, I asked her what would set her free from the concentration camp in her mind. Miranda thought and then told me she wanted to go to a different school, but her dad wouldn't let her. We talked about her being Daddy's little girl and how letting go of that phase of their relationship would be a stretch for both of them. Several days later, I spoke to her father and encouraged him to set his daughter free. He did so, and she changed schools, overcame her epilepsy, and is now a beautiful young lady teaching in New York City.

✧ ✧ ✧

To be tolerant in a family is to create breathing room for everyone. It is to keep an open mind and an open heart, and to support each member in journeying to a deeper, higher, and healthier sense of his or her whole self.

Your children are not there just to reflect your ideas back to you. Your parents are not there just to approve of every notion you have. And your siblings have their own way as well. If you think of your family as a kind of United Nations of personalities, then perhaps you can use a little patience and respect to transform your conflicts into true tolerance.

An intolerant heart is, in a sense, an unforgiving heart. Recently, I had a client I loved perhaps too much. Abe was a wandering Jew like myself, but his wandering included parents who divorced when he was six, and living as an adolescent and adult in England, Africa, Israel, and Italy. Abe had low self-esteem. His sense of self was frozen at that moment in time when his mother and father separated. He never had the opportunity to grieve the loss of his family unit. He was full of judgment toward his parents, especially his mother, whom he criticized as superficial, cold, and completely unprepared for motherhood. Abe took solace in orthodox Judaism, in which he became well versed. He turned out to be a scholar, a musician, and a student of the Kabbalah. When I met him, he was married to a wonderful woman, and they had adopted two beautiful children, a girl and a boy both from Brazil. His son was now six.

During his private sessions with me in Milan, Abe cried a lot whenever the issue of family came up. He tended to talk a lot about Judaism, sometimes turning his emotions away from his problems and speaking passionately about God, Israel, or the destruction of the temple, in particular. I supported Abe in writing letters to his parents, but he never would.

After a while, Abe came to a three-week program in the States. It was an excruciatingly hot summer. In the middle of the program he volunteered to work with another teacher, a psychiatrist, at the front of the room, demonstrating a technique that was instructional to the whole group. In the middle of the demonstration, Abe started to feel his rage toward his parents for the divorce. It was the first time I had seen him touch the anger instead of wallowing in his sadness and self-pity. One of his hands balled into a fist, which he waved in the air. Just as he was about to release the rage toward his parents, he transferred it completely and screamed, "Those bastards, they destroyed the temple!" When the instructor tried to bring Abe back to the destruction of the family, Abe would not go near his rage again. He deflected, intellectualized, and pushed all his emotions back into their familiar pigeonholes.

After the program, Abe returned to his family in Europe and, immediately, everything blew up. He had a huge row with his wife, who decided to divorce him. They went to a rabbi, then to Israel to finalize the separation, and he decided he would move back there. I saw him in Milan the day before he left for Tel Aviv. He said to me that it was so amazing how he was six when his parents divorced and that his own son was six now. I once again urged him to write letters to his parents.

Abe was stuck in intolerance toward his parents, feeling a complete inability to accept the divorce that happened when he was a child. In a sense, his soul was stuck at that point in time, especially in his judgment that the divorce was unjust, a judgment easily projected on the destruction of the temple, or any other injustice that he perceived in the world. He would never be free until he transformed this unforgiving position to a more tolerant view of his parents. To do this, he would have to contact and release the rage he touched on so briefly that hot summer day when he raised his fist in the air.

Abe had been led to the water, but he wasn't ready to drink.

FORGIVENESS ROAD

Make a list of the people you are intolerant of. Choose one with whom you are willing to transform your relationship. Close your eyes and imagine walking down Forgiveness Road with him or her. It is an incredibly beautiful spring evening and the fragrance of flowers fills the air. A gentle breeze blows, and the sun is setting brilliantly as you walk west. Surrounded by God's splendor, your heart opens and love replaces all grievances. Imagine saying you're sorry to this person, asking for his or her forgiveness, and taking each other's hand as you walk on. See the two of you come to a New Point of View, where you can look down Forgiveness Road to Empathy Valley. The view is magnificent, as you observe a virtual paradise below. You turn to your companion and you thank him or her for being your perfect teacher. Your heart overflows with gratitude.

As globalization homogenizes the world, the cry for separation is once again heard. Xenophobia has become a chronic disease in our society. People are once again afraid of their neighbors. Racial cleansing, civil war, terrorism, and plain old hatred continue to rock our civilization. As "foreigners" threaten the job security of "nationals," some people feel more and more resistance to inclusion, expansion, and tolerance. When the Berlin Wall came down, the world hailed the end of an era. When the USSR was dissolved, the democratic world cheered the end of the Cold War. But the results have been mixed at best, and discouraging too much of the time. As East Europeans poured into Western Europe, disrupting the job market, Westerners, feeling threatened, were seized with xenophobic feelings. They began to lose their livelihoods to people who would do their job for far less money. As Europe begins to embrace one currency and a more unified marketplace, individual nations, cultures, neighborhoods, and people wonder how much of their roots they must give up in the name of fostering a new global economy.

We cannot have true tolerance until we change the way we educate and govern. When teaching children that discovering their essential self-worth is as important as mastering math and science, then we will have made a good start. Having said that, in too many countries children are deprived of any meaningful education about self-esteem, relationships, and communication. If a child is not inspired with the love of learning, she will grow up into an adult blinded by ignorance. And we all know where ignorance leads. If a child's inherent curiosity is nurtured and stimulated, her mind will naturally open to new ideas and new ways. We need to teach the children of the world open-mindedness by making it a universal educational requirement. It is by planting the seeds of learning in the minds of our youth that we safeguard the future of the world.

Every child deserves to know her own value, develop her own natural talents, and learn the art of creating a successful small business or otherwise marketing herself in the global economy. Achieving these goals should be the primary purpose and function of education as well as governments through-out the world.

Until we empower children to lead the way, the collective journey home will be threatened by the animosity of our ancestors.

After two thousand years of Christianity, we still can't turn the other cheek very well, although we often look the other way. After five thousand years of Judaism, we still anticipate persecution and seek to persecute the persecutor beyond his ability to persecute us. And Islam seems to be the latest unfortunate breeding ground for viewing the world in terms of the faithful versus the infidels.

While tolerance does not mean embracing abuse, violence, or injustice, it does mean accepting others as we would have them accept us. So, the next time you are tempted to be intolerant of someone, imagine inviting that person to your dinner table, breaking bread with him, and sharing some soul food. In a civilized society, when a beggar, foreigner, or homeless vagabond enters town, we should all invite him in to share our good fortune and feast.

In the end, your tolerance of another is a blessing to you.

❖ ❖ ❖ ❖

As the new millennium dawned we were obsessed by the image of children, ostracized by their peers, bringing bombs and guns to schools and, all too often, using them. Then, on September 11, everything changed as grown-up children from faraway lands, fueled by ancient hatred and a need to show the world, made us forget that intolerance and terror were already gripping our nation from within.

It troubles me that, as I write, there have been two bomb scares in my twelve-year-old granddaughter's school during the last year. The first time, she called me and her voice was trembling. The second time she sounded calm. I realized she was becoming accustomed to the situation.

Who would do such a thing? A child feeling rejected? A victim of a bully? Or some smart-alecky kid thinking it was a cool way to get out of school early?

What troubles me more is the thought of multitudes of children around the world and elsewhere, deprived of their basic educational rights, and recruited by terrorist groups with fervent promises of a secure future.

Perhaps what terrifies me most, however, is the thought of millions of women throughout the world deprived of their fundamental human right to develop and express a healthy, educated sense of self, not to mention their right to basic pre- and perinatal care. Both studies and common sense tell us that where women and children are given a minimum of a good primary school education, then a healthy, stable, and tolerant society tends to emerge.

If we don't teach our women and children, what good is education? If we persecute whole segments of the population with ignorance, we all live in greater darkness.

Who then will carry the torch of universal tolerance on the journey to the future? Without it, where will there be light?

The Pitfall

The *pitfall* on the journey to tolerance is submission. If you think that being tolerant of others means accepting intolerable behavior, you are missing the point. For example, if you have an abusive husband but your self-esteem is so low you don't know you deserve better, you are in trouble. If you continue to submit to his abuse in the name of tolerance, you are deceiving yourself in the worst possible way. Some things we should never tolerate, such as abuse, murder, terrorism, genocide, racism, sexism, and discrimination of any sort. We should speak out against *all* human rights violations. And we should remove ourselves from situations in which we allow ourselves to be victims. On the other hand, if we fall into the very same hatred we are condemning, what have we accomplished that is of any real value? The challenge is to overcome the temptation to descend into violence while rising to the occasion, that is, having compassion and tolerance for the one who is misbehaving, knowing his pain must be deep indeed, but not stooping to tolerate his unethical actions. Be tolerant of the man, not his injustice. What Jesus meant by "turn the other cheek" was not only to avoid vengeance. He also implied that we should not look hatred in the eye because it could be contagious. So it was with Gandhi when he preached "passive resistance." He wasn't urging his people to be literally passive in the face of oppression. On the contrary, he was expressing the time-proven truth that patience, tolerance, and nonconfrontation are ultimately more active and efficient tools for transformation than retaliation. When you fight against injustice, injustice grows stronger. When you simply stand up to it, it becomes more visible, unacceptable, and powerless.

Steps on the Second Journey

1. Respect others.
2. Have the courage to leave your judgments behind.
3. Develop a new point of view.
4. Try to see things from other people's point of view.
5. Learn from others.
6. Walk down Forgiveness Road.
7. Celebrate diversity.
8. Understand that each person has a different history.
9. Look at your family as a melting pot, not hostile territory.
10. Where there is a difference of opinion, it's not always a matter of right and wrong.
11. Learn patience. Time can teach you open-mindedness.

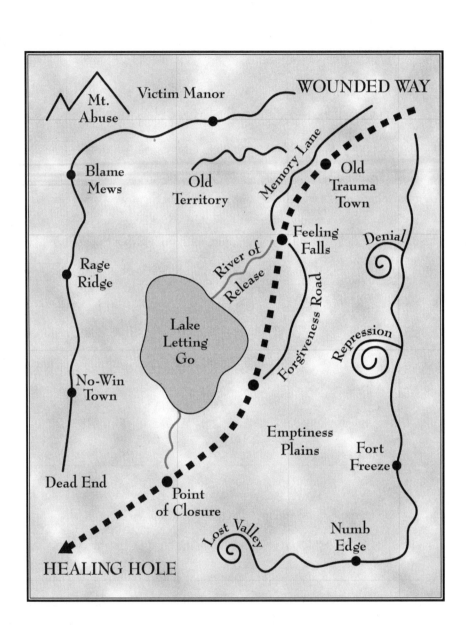

Journey 3

The Way of Healing Old Wounds

P art of the journey home is knowing where you came from. By
this I mean not only your roots but also the events that helped
form your sense of self. Some of these events were positive, others
painfully negative. To return to your whole self requires unraveling the painful memories like layers of an onion. Then you can
make peace with them.

As you begin your journey on this planet, you may suffer various shocks and traumas that freeze your soul at specific points in
time. Birth is often such a time, full of overwhelming sensation,
separation anxiety, loss of control, and painful physical manipulation. In my work, many clients journey back to their births on
their way home to themselves. Memories of abuse, disapproval,
and shame can also be holding you back from your complete self.
As can memories of a time when a loved one died or parents
divorced. The birth of a younger sibling can also be confusing to
a child who has been accustomed to being the center of attention.

The path you have traveled in this life is strewn with
wounded fragments of yourself. The pain was big and you were
little, unable to integrate what was going on at the time. It is never
too late to retrieve these lost parts of yourself, and in fact self-
retrieval is an essential journey on the road to self-actualization. All
you need to do is some backtracking.

Whatever is unresolved from your past lies buried beneath your conscious mind as well as in the cellular memory bank of your body. These memories can be accessed through a variety of techniques, and once you begin this journey your guides will appear to show you the appropriate way for you.

❖ ❖ ❖ ❖ ❖ ❖ ❖ ❖ ❖ ❖

Harrison was describing a memory. "I'm standing in a garden. I'm all alone. Maybe I'm five or six years old." He is sitting in a chair looking past me into space. Although in the middle of his life, his body has a distinctly childlike posture as he speaks. "I think I've done something wrong. But I haven't. I've been falsely accused." Harrison was working on the issue of feeling controlled and manipulated by powerful women. He felt very strongly that being with a woman would entail a loss of his freedom. "My mother's in the house and she's angry at me. She thinks I've been bad to my sister, but it's not true. I did nothing."

I asked Harrison if he could go into the house and find his mother. He did so. She was with his sister, and when she saw him she told him to go back to the garden until she said to come in. I could see Harrison's face change expression. He went from the sad little boy to the angry little boy. "I'm very angry with both of them. I feel they are trying to control me. I'm going back outside." I allowed him to follow his instincts. "I'm back outside in the garden. I love the flowers. But I am very angry at the women."

I suggested to Harrison that he make an *innervention*. I asked him to imagine his adult self joining the child in the garden. He had no trouble doing this. I told him to tell the boy he was innocent and that he had done nothing wrong. "Comfort him with words and hug him as well." Then I asked him to take the boy by the hand and go back into the house to explain things to his mother. "I can't," Harrison said. "I'm too angry and when I'm angry I prefer silence." I let him feel what he was saying and then asked him if it was he who was angry, or the child. "The child is angry, not me." "Go into the house with the child, Harrison, and let you, the adult, do the talking. Explain to your mother that she made a mistake and she is punishing the little boy for something he never did and that it is hurting him." He went deep within himself, tears streaming down his face. Finally, he opened his eyes and said, "I loved my mother so much, I would have stayed in that garden forever. Thank you. I feel more myself now."

HEALING OLD WOUNDS

The third journey toward a healthy sense of self is a journey to the past, a soul journey with the goal of healing old wounds. Unfortunately, many of us are damaged goods. As we were growing up we suffered certain shocks and traumas to our bodies and souls that caused us to separate from ourselves merely to survive.

The way of healing wounds takes you down Memory Lane to Feeling Falls, where you connect with old, unresolved feelings, which you can leave in the River of Release or Lake Letting Go. Eventually, you cross Emptiness Plains, where you experience the nothingness beneath old pain, and from there you arrive at Point of Closure and a feeling of wholeness.

I have many friends in AA. They are recovering alcoholics. What they are taught is that they are always in recovery and the process is never complete. Once an alcoholic, always an alcoholic. Many of them have not had a drink in ten, twenty years. Still, if you ask them, they will tell you they are in recovery, not recovered. I used to argue against this point of view, and to this day I have reservations. It feels like a heavy burden to carry through one's whole life, this fear of denial and an unchanging view of oneself. On the other hand, who can argue with success? The twelve-step program supported by Alcoholics Anonymous is a proven system for controlling alcoholism as well as substance abuse of any kind. In addition, when you have a chemical dependency on alcohol, even when you stop drinking the chemical addiction remains. So, in a sense, you do remain a recovering alcoholic even after you have recovered from the habit itself.

Maybe we are all in endless recovery, but I don't think so. I am not happy with what I perceive to be an increasing addiction to healing in the New Age. I agree with Caroline Myss, who perceived that healing should have closure. For me the idea that life itself is a healing process makes too many unsupported presumptions. If the purpose of life is healing, then we must all be wounded from the beginning. But not everyone is. Many people are healthy individuals, unscarred and unscathed, living fairly harmonious lives. Also, the notion that life is about healing resembles a modern twist on the belief that life is about penance. Some people insist that we are born sinners and if we do proper penance we get to go to the "good place" after we

31

die. The New Age version is that we are born traumatized and if we devote our lives to recovery, we get to go to a higher plane afterward. Same story, new words.

When Christina came for her ninth session with me, she curled up into a ball on the couch and began to cry. I asked her what was going on, and she replied that her husband was neglecting her just like her father did when she was a child. Then she began to vent her rage toward her father, who never acknowledged her, recognized her accomplishments, or supported her. She screamed, pounded the cushions, and had a good old-fashioned temper tantrum. I let her go on and on for a while, then commented that I thought she was covering old territory, but that if she really believed there was something new to discover I was willing to go there with her. She paused, then smiled. She said no, there was nothing new, but it wouldn't go away. I pointed out that it wouldn't go away because she kept going there.

I have seen this sort of behavior fairly frequently. People revisit old territory in their healing sessions simply because it is familiar and therefore secure, however miserable. When a client repeats the same memories with one therapist, it is fairly easy to catch and change the behavior. But often the client takes his bag of wounds from one healer to another, from one technique to another, never letting go of the bag. It is as though her journey in life cannot proceed without the same old bag.

MEMORY LANE

Think of a problem you have—a conflict in a relationship or a disappointment at work. Define how you feel about the problem, then take a walk down Memory Lane. Remember other times when you felt a similar way, or found yourself in similar situations. Go back to the earliest similar memory you can find and see what was happening at that time. Now imagine yourself as the adult you now are, intervening in the situation and standing up for the "other you," confronting anyone who might have been unfair to you and correcting any conflict or misunderstanding that might have been happening. Finally, envision your current self and your remembered self going off together somewhere safe and serene, and hearing your current self tell the "other you" everything you needed to hear back then when you suffered shock.

Recently, a friend of mine in Italy asked a very simple but very important question: how do you let go? Before I answer it, however, I'd like to address the issue of how to access and retrieve the lost parts of yourself. First, you dig, then you dump.

There are many ways to go back in your mind. You can use traditional forms of psychoanalysis and therapy. Hypnosis is another tool. Regression can work. Breathwork also can help. Even controlled LSD sessions have been used as a means of accessing buried memories. It is important to realize, however, that what is remembered is *not* what happened. In fact, when a trauma happens, there is a perception of what is happening. The perception may or may not be accurate. Even if it is accurate, it is still distorted by the observer, who participates in the creation of the memory he is storing. Years later, when he recalls the memory, he is observing the memory through a new observer, his current complex persona who is looking back in time. So a memory is, in a sense, a distortion of a distortion. I'm referring to a normal memory. There are also instances of false memory syndrome.

I once had a client who insisted she had been abused by her father, but I never felt the truth of her case. Finally, in one session, she recalled having the fantasy of sex with her father. She realized that her memory of abuse was actually the memory of the wish, rather than the fact.

How do you let go? Well, sometimes a person can just drop an issue in the moment. One moment he is furious, the next he's released it. Of course, you have to be careful he is not just slyly repressing it. Other times, a person regresses to the incident, feels what she needs to feel, and finds her closure. *A Course in Miracles* advises you to practice "selective remembering," recalling only the loving thoughts and forgetting the rest. Another way is the "soul retrieval" technique practiced by shamans. Some people use the affirmation technique, drawing a vertical line down the center of a page, then writing a positive affirmation on the left side and any negative response on the right. There is also Dr. Stephen Wolinsky's process of dismantling the false identities, then reabsorbing them into your essence. However you let go, it is necessary to face the emptiness that replaces whatever was filling it up previously. The emptiness is where you actually return to the source of your being. Out of nothing comes you!

I should mention that there are no guarantees with any form of therapy or healing technique. Different paths work for different people. Sometimes, nothing seems to work. And other times people who have had the worst births, suffered from abuse, and grew up without many positive influences bounce back and seem to be healthy normal adults. The resiliency of the human spirit can be amazing.

Some of my professional colleagues feel that anyone not involved with healing is in denial. I think that's a fairly narrow-minded view. Besides, even if it is true, so what? Who are we to judge what enables others to carry on in this life? In fact, sometimes denial is more healing than feeling the pain. Dr. Larry Dossy reports on a study showing that a patient who suffers a heart attack is more likely to survive if he denies it, pretending it's just a minor pain, than if he is brought into the hospital terrified because he knows he has had a heart attack. Go figure!

A mother and two of her grown daughters attended one of my seminars. One of the sisters shared that there were three sisters in all and that two of them, the two in the room, had been repeatedly raped by the father as children. The third, the youngest, was never touched. The two abused sisters went through therapy, recovered, were married with children of their own, and found themselves living fairly normal lives. The third sister went mad. She thought there was something terribly wrong with her because Daddy didn't love her the way he loved her sisters. She ended up permanently institutionalized. Who can say for sure what causes the most trauma? Events outside ourselves? Or our own interpretations of those events?

Recovery is a tricky road. You can never really say for certain whether you have recovered completely or not. Ten years ago a dear friend of mine died in Bali when his ultralight plane crashed, killing him and the pilot. Since he had virtually no family, we cremated him, did ceremonies, I threw his ashes into the Indian Ocean, and when we came home I went through a year of fairly deep and extensive mourning. I thought I had put it behind me. Then, one day ten years later, I was sharing about an apparently pleasant dream I had the night before when suddenly all the grief came storming back as if I had never shed a tear at all. Was I needlessly revisiting old territory? Was I touching a part of my grief that I had left untouched? Was I really sad about some other loss and transferring it to this memory? Who can say?

What about a person whose father dies and he feels nothing and then he loses his dog and all that unexpressed emotion comes pouring out? Has he mourned his father successfully, vicariously, through his dog? What if he even denies the grief has been transferred from father to dog? What if he really did love his dog more than his father? We can have our opinion, personal or professional, but we can never say for sure.

It is important to remember that we have a natural ability to heal ourselves without even knowing it. Sometimes I ask a group, "How many of you have ever healed yourself?" Usually a few hands go up. Then, when I ask, "How many of you have ever been sick and then recovered?" Everyone raises their hand. We are recovering all the time, only we usually don't acknowledge it. We heal from physical damage and we heal from spiritual damage. Whether we heal consciously or unconsciously, medically or spontaneously, doesn't really matter. The significant thing is that we get well again.

So it is with recovery. You can recover through consciously choosing a form of therapy that seems to work for you. You can recover by letting nature take its course, or with the help of hypnosis, drugs, or even denial. Sometimes you heal in your dreams. A friend calls this "night school." You work things out when your conscious mind is resting. You wake up, you feel healed, and maybe you don't even know why or how. Recovery can happen invisibly. Often, a client will have a breathing session that is energetic but uneventful, then report afterward that a major problem has been resolved. You don't have to examine everything that went wrong to make things right.

Understanding everything does not necessarily heal. Many people go through years of psychoanalysis, spend huge amounts of money, and come to understand why they are so miserable. Have they recovered? No. They just understand where their misery comes from. Others can recover in one miraculous flash. We tend to mistrust quick fixes, especially those of us who have gone through long training to help people. We mistrust quick fixes as we condemn fast food. Yet it must be said that there is no law that recovery has to take a certain amount of time. My AA friends say you never recover, while students of *A Course in Miracles* say healing happens in one "holy instant." Perhaps they are both right. I am not here to tell you how to recover the missing pieces of your soul. If you are reading this book, I feel confident that you will be guided to the appropriate person or path.

◇ ◇ ◇ ◇

Dora wanted to quit smoking. She also had another problem, or two. She was in love with a married man and didn't want to talk about it. So I kept my mouth shut and my ears open. We traced her history of smoking back to her childhood. Her father smoked cigars and would occasionally let his little princess puff on one. She confided in me that she still liked to smoke a cigar now and then in the privacy of her own home. Her preference in public was cigarettes. As she began to see that her smoking habit was connected to her love for her father, she became more and more agitated. Then she remembered a time she had quit smoking for several months. When I asked her what happened, she simply said, "Oh, my God." Suddenly, she was crying, out of nowhere, and at the same time trying to talk her way out of it. I told her to breathe. The memory flashed before her eyes. She was in a hotel room. She had accompanied her father on a business trip, which she often did. She was about twenty at the time. Her father died suddenly in his sleep. She then went into complete shock. "I was in the room, but I wasn't there. I don't know where I was. I remember they took his body away. People were being very nice to me. I hadn't smoked in three months. Then someone handed me a cigarette and I lit up, not even thinking about it. I've been smoking ever since."

For Dora, simply remembering when she became frozen in time seemed to be enough for at least a partial recovery. She didn't quit smoking after our session, but, ironically, her relationship with the married man, who was her business partner, changed. She told him she did not want to continue to be the other woman in his life, nor did she want to support his infidelity and consequential guilt. She asked him to choose. He did. He separated from his wife, began divorce proceedings, and he and Dora now were looking for a home together. Incidentally, he's a smoker too.

❖ ❖ ❖ ❖

When you are on the road to recovery, whether it's long and winding, grueling and grinding, or seemingly unending, it is extremely helpful to retain your sense of humor. Becoming dreadfully serious about your own healing process generates added anxiety that is both counterproductive and unnecessary. It's hard enough when you are going through something difficult not to add additional weight to the process. Lighten up. Get away from the process now and then. Often, I advise a client to go to a comic movie to laugh or to a horror film to scream. Once, Mallie was stuck in a terrible rut. I don't remember what she was processing, but it was dragging her down to the bottom of the barrel. Finally, I couldn't take it any more, so I suggested we go to an Ingmar Bergman double feature, *Persona* and *Hour of the Wolf*. At first she thought I was crazy, but when we walked out after viewing these two brilliantly depressing movies, she was laughing, realizing that her problems paled in comparison to those of the characters in the Swedish master's dark imagination.

❖ ❖ ❖ ❖

Many people share a belief that "forgiveness is the key to happiness." While this may or may not be true for everyone, what seems obvious is that we are not always able to forgive completely on demand. In other words, sometimes we have to take the time to smell our anger, hurt, and feelings of betrayal on Forgiveness Road. In fact, giving yourself the time and space to feel everything you need to feel might make forgiveness extraneous.

Joan was a bodybuilder. She was a beautiful woman obsessed with being fit. I met her at a seminar in Argentina. She was feeling a lot of pressure to forgive her father for having sexually abused her as a child. When I asked her where all this pressure came from, she said it was peer pressure from her spiritual community. When I asked her to close her eyes, take a breath, and tell me where she felt this pressure, she did so and told me the pressure was around her heart. I asked her to describe the pressure and she reported that it felt like a cold piece of steel. Then I suggested she peel away the steel like Velcro and tell me what was underneath. "Fear," she whispered. "Absolute terror." As she dialogued with her fear, she came to see her truth, namely that the pressure to forgive her father was covering her fear of being abused again. As long as she held onto the pressure, she didn't have to face her fear.

I asked Joan to create two forms for her feelings: one, the Joan under pressure, and two, the Joan who was afraid. The first became a female knight in a suit of armor. She named the knight "The Protector." The second became "Red Jell-O." She then walked across the room, first as the knight and then as the Jell-O. I told Joan she could play either of these parts, whenever either was most appropriate. When she asked me if she still had to forgive her father, I replied, "Who wants to know? The Protector or Red Jell-O?" We had a good laugh, she went home, and the issue of forgiving her father disappeared.

POINT OF CLOSURE

Think of someone with whom you feel incomplete, someone whose presence causes you discomfort. It can be a family member, an old lover with whom you are unresolved, or a business associate. It can be someone alive or dead. When you've chosen someone, imagine this person standing in front of you and complete the following statements to him or her. (1) "Something I've been upset about is _____"; (2) "Something I want to forgive you for is _____"; (3) "Something I want to forgive myself for is _____"; (4) "Something I'm grateful to you for is _____"; (5) "Something I need to tell you in order to feel complete with you is _____." Imagine yourself embracing this person.

You can leave a part of yourself behind in your life without even knowing it. Jenny did. She was thirty-three years old, but had a *little girl act* that was quite evident in her body language and giggle. When she was three, her father, whom she adored, died. Her mother did not know how to talk about death, so she told Jenny that "Daddy went away on a very long trip." In the little girl's mind, it was clear that one day Daddy would return from his very long trip. So Jenny put a part of herself on hold, waiting for him. Meanwhile, her body grew up, her mind grew up. Intellectually, she now knew that her father was dead and would never come back. When she came to me, however, she shared that she was unable to sustain a relationship for more than three years. The man would abandon her, she would reject him, or, as had just happened, the man went on a very long trip to Australia and never came back. Jenny thought there might be some connection with her father.

In her first session, Jenny kept drifting off, and when I asked her where she was going, she said far away but she didn't know where. In her second session, she stayed in present time but felt very angry and didn't know why. It was in her third session that she began to have memories of her father and cried. Her soul seemed to wail from a vast hollowness within. In the following session I asked her if she could remember the moment when her mother told her about her father's long trip. "Yes," she said, "I'm there now." She saw herself as a three-year-old, her mother kneeling to be at eye level with her. She said her mom was crying. "I feel so confused. I am so angry at Mommy for lying. But I am sad about Daddy going away. And I feel so bad for my mommy at the same time." She began to cry like a three-year-old. I allowed her to feel all this, then suggested she do an *innervention*.

I asked her to imagine herself entering the scene as the adult she now was. "I'm there," she said. I instructed her to take the child into her arms and tell her exactly what she needed to hear to feel closure on this situation. After a while, Jenny reported to me, "I'm telling the child that her daddy has died and will never come back. The child is calling me a liar, telling me her daddy went away and is coming back. I'm telling her, no, that's not the truth. I'm so sorry. . . . Now she is crying. . . . . Poor little girl. I'm saying that her daddy will love her always even though he can't be with her anymore."

I told her to shift her attention to her mother and tell her what she needed to say to feel closure. Her face became twisted. "I am so angry at my mom." "Is it you or the child who is angry, Jenny?" She thought about it. "It's the child. She feels so betrayed." She took her time. "I've told my mother she was wrong to do that, that it was a bad influence on me, and although I have been angry for years without knowing it, I can now forgive her."

After retrieving the part of her self that had been frozen at age three, Jenny's entire manner changed completely. She realized that her little-girl act had been a way of holding onto her father and even trying to seduce men into *being* her father. Then, when a relationship called for two adults to participate responsibly, she would be totally lost. Eventually, Jenny recovered, found a great man, and was able to sustain a spiritually, emotionally, intellectually, sexually, and psychologically mature relationship.

One thing that helps me to retrieve myself is to remember who is looking for whom. Yes, I am trying to recover the missing pieces of myself. But I am also the one looking for myself. I am *not* the lost pieces. I think of myself sometimes as a detective searching for clues, talking to witnesses, retracing the steps of the missing person, who happens to be me, or maybe a client or student. But just as beauty is in the eye of the beholder, when you are seeking self-realization you are, in fact, the one seeking, not the one sought. That is why when you recover from the damage done to your developing self, you realize you were there all along, perhaps locked up in some internal closet, attic, or basement, but home nonetheless.

So it is that recovery is a journey home and, when you arrive, you open the door and greet yourself.

The Pitfall

The *pitfall* on the way to recovery is becoming overly enamored of the healing process. You can be as addicted to healing as to painkillers—a "heal-aholic." To be chronic about healing is as disturbing as to experience a chronic illness itself. To identify yourself with your recovery rather than your health is a misrepresentation of who you are. You are not your wounds, scars, or traumas. I remember in the '60s, President Lyndon Johnson pulling up his shirt and revealing a huge appendix scar on his body. How ludicrous to identify yourself by your wounds and scars! How counterproductive to think that you are worthy of attention primarily because of what's wrong with you! If you are on the path of recovery, remember that the journey has a beginning, middle, and end. There *is* closure. Wellness *will* come. And when it does, you had better be prepared to reveal your magnificence with as much enthusiasm, passion, and conviction that you used to promote your wounds. Prepare for wellness along the way. Take time out from your journey. Play. Enjoy. Celebrate the wonder of it all. Go roll in the mud.

Steps on the Third Journey

1. Become aware of emotional patterns in your life.
2. Remember where you came from.
3. Don't get stuck in old territory.
4. You are an adult, not an inner child.
5. Learn how to let go.
6. Forgive at your comfort level.
7. Relax into the emptiness underneath the pain.
8. Try to keep a sense of humor.
9. Find a point of closure.
10. Take time out from healing.
11. Remember, you can't change the past.

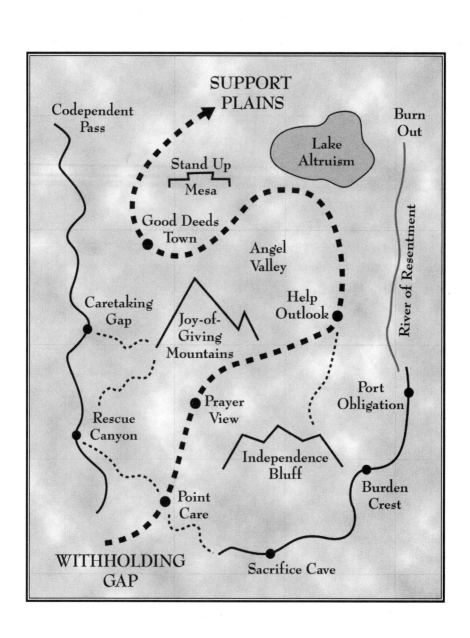

Journey 4

The Path of Extended Support

We all need support on the journey home. Alone, the journey can be difficult and treacherous, with twists and turns along the way. Whether we are laboring down the back road of healing or standing atop the cliffs of tolerance, we all can use a helping hand or someone to lean on. What is equally important, if perhaps less obvious, is that to actualize ourselves we all need to extend support.

Extending support is a process of expanding our souls and strengthening our spirits. Making the journey a solitary one might seem to be taking the more romantic road, but in the end going at it solo is too much of an ego trip to bring you home to your whole self. Of course, there is a proper time and place to express an independent spirit, but independence is not the end of the journey, just another step on the path.

When you stretch to support another person on his journey, you receive multiple benefits.

You experience your value to others, your ability to make a difference, and the satisfaction of selfless giving. You learn the magic of love in action. As you approach home, you realize that you are part of a larger family and you are not the only one searching in the wilderness.

The key to extending support so that it enriches you and soothes others is to do it for the joy it brings to your heart, not for some future payback. To support in order to obligate is to veer off course at the crossroads of love and control. Extend yourself because it is your nature to do so, whereas fear and contraction diminish the light of your soul.

Look for the guiding signs, and you will meet the people who need your support as surely as the right people will be sent to support you. In the end, whether you're on the giving or receiving end of a helping hand, your journey is aided by those you touch along the way.

◇ ◇ ◇ ◇ ◇ ◇ ◇ ◇ ◇ ◇

One morning Mallie wakes up with a dreadful cold. I feel so bad for her. The only thing I can think about is how to help her recover as quickly as possible. I ask her if there is anything she wants; she grunts. I offer to make her tea, toast, eggs; she groans. Granola? She rolls her eyes. I ask if she wants some vitamins, *Echinacea,* food supplements; she snarls. Finally, I say, "Is there anything I can do to support you?" She looks at me and replies in no uncertain terms, "Just leave me alone!"

Mallie later comes downstairs sniffling. I want to make all her symptoms disappear. She begins to do a load of laundry and I offer to do it instead. She brushes me off. Then she opens the refrigerator and takes out the eggs. "I'd be happy to make you breakfast," I offer cheerfully. She says she prefers doing it herself. After breakfast she goes upstairs, bathes, and dresses. When she comes down, she announces she is going to the office for a couple of hours. I urge her to take the day off. She is sick, after all. "It's only a cold. I'm fine," she replies, popping some homeopathic pills into her mouth. "By the way, can you fold the sheets when the dryer's done?" "Sure," I respond, eager to support her any way I can. "I love you." "I know," she says, smiling.

I pick up the phone to call Mallie at the office. I hear her stuffed head as she speaks into the receiver. "Hi, honey," I say, "how's it going?" She sniffles and responds, "I've had better days." "I want to help so badly," I tell her. "Why don't you come home and I'll run you a hot bath?" "Nah," she replies, "I'll be fine." "Yeah, but you got to take care of yourself, baby." She comes back at me. "I *am* taking care of myself. This is the way I do it. You know me by now." I take a deep breath. "I'm just worried about you." "What's to worry? You've never had a cold?"

Mallie comes home from the office late in the afternoon. I have called her three more times to find out how she is feeling. Once she sniffled, once she coughed, and once she sneezed over and over. Each time, she said she was okay, it was just a cold. When I tried to insist she come home, she suggested I get a life. Now, as she walks in, she looks somewhat the worse for wear. She refolds the sheets on the dryer, my folds not quite meeting her standards. In the past, I might have taken exception to this correction, but by now we know each other well enough just to laugh. We embrace. She asks for a glass of white wine and I pour two. I tell her how much I love her and how bad I feel for her. She smiles and says she'll be better tomorrow. I tell her that I feel so frustrated by my inability to support her in any way. She laughs and reminds me that she was a forceps birth and that hands-on support brings up nightmares of control, manipulation, and pain. I say I know, but I just want to find some vehicle for transporting my love to her. She takes a breath and says that I have done that. She says, "Your love makes all the difference."

What does supporting others have to do with the journey toward a healthy sense of self? Plenty. But, to comprehend the connection, we first must get clear on what support really is. And to know what it is, we first must see what it is not.

Support, like forgiveness, charity, and cooperation, is one of the most misunderstood virtues in the world. Traditionally, to offer support has meant to stand behind someone or something you believe in, or to lend a helping hand to someone in need. According to Webster's dictionary, to support is (1) "to endure bravely or quietly, to bear"; (2) "to promote the interests or cause of"; (3) "to uphold or defend as valid"; and (4) "to assist or help," among other things. According to these definitions, you can support an idea, a cause, or a person. Whatever you choose to support, however, the assumption is that when you are in a position of support, you bear a burden, as when a foundation supports a building, a man his family, or a wife her husband. Support implies sacrifice. It connotes that the one giving support is putting his own interests on the back burner to support the interests of someone or something separate. I beg to differ.

THE PATH OF EXTENDED SUPPORT

Support begins at Point Care. Once you realize how deeply you care about another human being, you naturally want to reach out to her in her hour of need. It is in your nature to do so, and honoring your nature stretches your being. The challenge is to stay on the path of extended support rather than veer off toward Sacrifice Cave and Burden Crest on the one hand or Rescue Canyon and Caretaking Gap on the other. True support guides you to caregiving through Prayer View, Help Outlook, and Good Deeds Town. In the end you find there is no separation between extending a helping hand and receiving one yourself.

Who would imagine that offering support could be one of the most mystical journeys on the road to self-realization? On the contrary, most people would agree with the dictionary. Look at money, for example. Parents bear the financial burden of raising children, and the staggering figure of raising a child to independence is undeniable. Until recently, in our culture the burden fell mostly on the father's shoulders to support both wife and children, although in the last fifty years, as women have claimed their freedom outside the home, more and more women have made their financial sacrifice to the skyrocketing cost of raising children and supporting a household.

You're walking down the street. A homeless person extends his palm and says, "Can you support me with a quarter for a cup of coffee?" This question is the same in theory as the Third World country that asks the superpower to support its economic development: "Can you support us with $50 million to help us develop our infrastructure?" The implication is that those who *have* should give some support to those who have not, whether a parent to a child, a prosperous person to a needy one, or a rich country to a poor one. It's logical. Charity, generosity, the Christian/Jewish/Muslim/Hindu/Buddhist way. No?

We also pay taxes to support our country. We bear the burden of our government's budget and national debt. Why? Our country is not our child. It is not a poor person on the street. And it is not an underdeveloped nation, nor are you and I superpowers. Why do we support our government?

Not only do we financially support our country, we are so kind as to financially support our banks. Think about it. You may beg your bank for a loan or a mortgage, but where does the bank's basic support come from? We, the people! In a sense, a bank borrows the money we deposit, paying us a nominal amount of interest, then invests our money so as to return a much larger interest rate to itself. We are the bank's bank, supporting the institution that seems to provide us with support, or not. Once again, we bear the burden. Why are we such masters of self-sacrifice? Where is this journey taking us?

We all give a lot, and we tend to feel we give a lot more than we get. Often, we keep score and end up feeling ripped off, by our government for misusing our money, by our banks for exploiting us, even by our children for not appreciating how much we give.

Think about it. Why should we bear the brunt? Why should we make the sacrifice? Are we all financial martyrs, would-be saints, casting a huge percentage of our incomes to the wasteful policies of our government, then feeling angry at the bum on the street who asks for a handout? Sometimes it seems as though we ourselves are not so very far removed from that homeless vagabond.

The truth about support is that, if we look at it as I have been describing it, we are fully entitled to resent the ones we support and rebel against the very notion of support. But support is not really about anything outside ourselves. The reason to support another human being is not that you have and he needs, but rather that you need to share what you have in order to journey toward your greater self. The spiritual, and material, consequence of sharing freely is expansion. Withholding produces contraction. Another way of saying this is, love generates growth while fear stunts it.

With money it's easy to see why we need to keep it moving, since money has value only in circulation. In other words, if you put all your money in a closet and never touch it, you have a bunch of paper with ink in your closet, and that's all. If you circulate money wisely, it increases in value. Even when you deposit money in a bank, you are circulating it because the bank invests it.

But beyond that, the one you give to is the medium by which you expand your own consciousness. When you extend yourself, you grow. When you extend your soul through love, charity, generosity, or support, your soul is uplifted by that extension. In a sense, the one you give to is your greater self. Until you give, you tend to see the other person as an outsider, not connected to your soul. It's a challenge in today's world to feel the interconnectedness of all life. We understand the truth about ecology and how we are all part of one biosystem. But there is a vast difference between our understanding the essential unity of life and practicing that truth in our daily relationships.

PRAYER VIEW

Imagine coming to Prayer View, an overlook where your prayers have extra energy and effectiveness. Now think of a person you really care about. Not someone you want to take care of, but someone you really care for. Feel that energy of caring well up inside you like a great ball of light. Think of your friend, feel the ball of light in you, and focus on a prayer of support for this special person in your life. After several minutes, repeat to yourself these words, "Joy to you, my friend."

Beatrice was a wealthy lady who resented supporting her husband, Oscar. He was an artist who didn't make money, and she felt used. In her mind, Oscar didn't really love her; he loved his art. She saw herself as his patron or sponsor rather than the love of his life. When they came to me for a session, the tension between them was almost palpable. Beatrice came from old wealth, all on her mother's side. Her dad was a gigolo who married her mom, took what he could get, and left her with a daughter, namely Beatrice. She was afraid the same thing would happen to her. Oscar also came from a wealthy family, but he had rejected his father's riches, preferring his own art to his father's "art" of manipulating him through money. He confessed that he felt terrible about the situation and wanted to support Beatrice. He called her his one and only love, his muse, his soul mate, and he began to cry as he shared his fear of losing her.

In Oscar's private session, he realized that he had decided never to receive money from someone who loved him. His memory of his father abusing him as a child by threatening to "cut him out" of the family fortune was so painful that he had unconsciously cut himself off from wealth. He wondered if his decision as a child was somehow sabotaging his success in both his marriage and his career. I had him do an *innervention,* revisiting a scene where his father was attacking him, then bringing Oscar's adult in as a protector of the child and peacemaker with his father. Afterward, Oscar said he was ready to forgive his father.

I then met with Beatrice alone. She asked me what she should do to help Oscar get on his financial feet. I asked her if she loved him and she replied, yes, more than anything. "More than all the money in the world?" I queried. She looked at me quizzically, not knowing where I was leading her. "Yes," she finally said. "Money is useless to me, really. I feel a slave to it. And I don't care about it at all." Tears streamed down her cheeks. I said to her, "Beatrice, you are a beautiful woman and your husband is obviously crazy about you. You are his love and his inspiration. He is not your father. I cannot tell you how to handle your money. That is your business alone. I can only tell you this: If you don't trust Oscar with your money, how will you ever trust him with your heart?" She gave me that quizzical look again. "Are you saying I should give him my money?" I shrugged my shoulders.

Some time later when I saw Beatrice and Oscar, they were a healed couple. She had put her fortune in both their names and he was selling paintings. "But that's not the reason we're happy," Oscar said. "No," Beatrice added, "we're happy because we're in love."

◇ ◇ ◇ ◇

When I give to that beggar in the street, I am giving to a part of myself. "I am involved in mankind," wrote John Donne. "No man is an island." Instead of distancing myself from the abhorrent image of poverty, I embrace that needy part of me as surely as the healing power of my body rushes to help a broken limb, should I have one. If a river in Germany is badly polluted, why should I care about it if I live in the USA? Because that river runs into some bay that opens onto some ocean that supports the quality of my life on this, my planet. That river runs through *me*. That beggar runs through me. That bank runs through me.

Of course, support is more than a financial issue. Our ability to give and receive emotional support is vital to the health of all our relationships. A good parent, for example, knows how to support a child without sabotaging him. Sometimes I see a mother smothering her child with love and attention. She will do everything for that child—make his bed, cook and clean up, dress the child, tie his shoelaces. The kid is maybe eight years old. He needs to be learning to take care of some of his own needs as well as contributing to the smooth running of family life and the home. Children should be raised to support themselves and their household rather than trained to expect the world to take care of them. For a home to be healthy the family should see itself as a team cooperating for the greater success of all members. Besides, if a parent does everything for a child, that child grows up with a strong pattern of helplessness, expecting anyone who loves him to make his bed, do his dishes, and, yes, even tie his shoelaces. It is important to remember that the job of parenting is not one of perennial caretaking, but, rather, of guiding a child toward greater independence. The process of weaning begins when the cord is cut at birth and continues gradually until the day that child has grown up and is prepared to leave home and fend for

49

himself. When that day comes, the parent is able to measure her own success by the fact that her child no longer needs her.

During the first year of life, things are different. An infant needs to attach to his mother especially, but to all members of the family as well. This form of support creates the security that promotes independence later on. So when your baby cries, pick him up. Let him sleep in your bed. Carry him. Breast-feed him. Massage him. Don't worry about spoiling him. You're just giving him more inner strength that will pay off in the future.

I often hear a parent say to a child, "I want you to cooperate!" While cooperation in the spiritual sense can express high-quality support and creativity, what does the parent mean when he asks for a child to cooperate with him, or with the child's siblings? Usually, he means that he wants the child to submit his will to that of someone else. So, the fine art of cooperation is reduced to *do it my way!* Submit. To the extent that supporting someone implies submission, nobody in his right mind wants to do it. If you have to be a slave to the person you are supporting, or cooperating with, you will resent that person for abusing his power over you.

Support only makes sense when you can see that supporting the other person supports you as well.

True support is not always what it looks like. Think about a friend. When do you feel supported by him? Is it when you have a rough day at work, go to a bar for some beers with him, complain about your boss, and his response is that he knows what you mean, his boss is a jerk too, and life sucks anyway. Is this support? Is this friendship? Or is this just a case of misery loves company? When someone really supports you, he might say something like "Well, if you really hate your job, why don't you stop complaining and start looking for a better one? You deserve to be happy at work!" Sometimes support should push you forward, not just give you something old and familiar to fall back on.

In a relationship, support can seem like sacrifice, but it really doesn't have to be. I have friends, a couple, Ben and Libby, and Libby tends to complain that Ben doesn't support her because he prefers a good football game on TV. I once talked to him about this issue. I suggested he make a list of his priorities and choose where to devote his time based on his personal preferences. He was surprised to discover that Libby was on the top of his list and football near the bottom. Then he began to support Libby more and more, feeling joy instead of resentment. When you support someone you love, you are not sacrificing, because you are selecting what you value more above what you value less. As your value system develops, your preferences change and you might have to remind yourself that you are only sacrificing less for more.

Supporting elderly parents is another aspect worth considering. Even at ninety-five, my mother was a feisty and fiercely independent spirit. As she aged, my sister and I tried to support her more and more. At first it seemed that we needed to create an entire support system for her, be it a retirement community or an assisted living situation. She would not hear of it. In her mind, she could take care of herself and had been doing so since she was thirteen and that was that! We felt she was in denial about her declining body and pushed for her to have more support. The more we tried to support her, however, the more she fought us tooth and nail until finally she insisted firmly that she didn't want to talk about it again.

We backed off. The thought of her in her mid-nineties living by herself in an apartment in New York City appalled us. But, slowly, we chose to look at the situation in a new light. Maybe Mom was right. Maybe her soul, her deep sense of herself, knew that her longevity was attached to her independence, and knew that to eliminate the latter would threaten the former. Who can say what support really is in such cases?

As I write, Mom is ninety-six, still living in her Chelsea apartment, surrounded by familiar objects and fond memories, and also supported by two very wonderful nurse's aides. Her dignity is safeguarded.

Edith is Mallie's mother. She suffers from Alzheimer's disease and resides in a nursing home in Vermont. For me, helping Mallie to support her has been a journey full of heartbreak, setbacks, and wonderful surprises. For years Mallie has made the journey back and forth to Vermont every other week. For a while, Edith's condition was fairly stable, but she began to deteriorate rapidly when the nursing home decided it would be wise to establish a separate wing for Alzheimer's patients. Surrounded only by people losing their minds, Edith began to lose her words, memories, and connection with present time. Eventually, she hardly recognized her own daughter.

One day Mallie went to visit and discovered that her mom's doctor had not seen her in nine months (even though he was required by law to see her every two months). At the same time, the nursing home was implementing another brilliant idea—a nonstimulation policy toward Alzheimer's patients. Mallie and I became incensed. We know that her mom loves and responds to music, dance, colors, movies, stories—activity. Moreover, we feel that the brain of anyone, be it an unborn child or a fading adult, responds to positive stimulation.

We researched our theory on the Internet and elsewhere, collecting articles, studies, and information to support our point of view. We wrote to the governor, attorney general, state senator, and representative—sending all our supporting material, and complaining. Very quickly, it seemed as if the entire state of Vermont responded to our stimulation. The governor and attorney general informed us that an investigation had started. Within one month our claims were validated and changes were made.

A few days ago, Mallie and I were discussing what had happened. "You know," she said, "this might not help Mom at all—she is probably too far gone. But in some invisible way I feel like the spirit of my mother has helped bring about changes that will support others."

Sometimes people don't want your support. They are suspicious of it, feeling that you are manipulating them, expecting something in return down the road. "Back off" is the message. Think of all the times you yourself resisted support.

Ambivalence toward support can go straight back to your birth, when your delivery team—your first support team—hurt you in the name of helping you. There you were, a completely helpless little body, perhaps turned, twisted, pulled, yanked, flipped over, and spanked. You might have been drugged by anesthesia, blinded by bright lights, frightened by loud noise, and humiliated by rough handling. On top of it all, you could very well have had your umbilical cord abruptly cut only to be separated from your mother and put in a nursery. All this was done to you by the first people who supported you in this life. The cellular memories of being jerked around tend to linger.

We all need support. Just as you go through periods of healing and recovery in your life, so do others. It is a challenge to learn how to support those you care about when they are going through their healing process. Not everyone wants it the same way. You need to learn flexibility and creativity in supporting each and every person you love. It does not work to impose your image of support on others because, in all probability, they have their own image. Some people like hands-on support. If so, rub their shoulders. Give them a hug. Take them out to lunch. Be a good listener. Others prefer support from a distance. So drop them a card. Pray for them. Give them a call. Send them flowers. If you are having difficulty lending support to someone, a good idea is to ask the person directly how she would like you to support her. This works especially well for those who fear that supports means control. If you allow the person to choose her own form of support, then she can feel in control of the support you are giving her.

HELP OUTLOOK

Tomorrow, as you go through your day, be aware of three people who could benefit from your support. These should be people who do not need you and whom you do not need to help, but people you could and would enjoy supporting. One by one, ask each person how you might support them. It could be a man carrying a heavy load, a girl trying to thread a needle, or an old lady crossing the street. If the person doesn't want your support, ask if he's sure before moving on to someone else.

Another aspect of support is knowing when to stand behind something or someone. You may think to stand behind implies being second fiddle, as in the stereotype of a woman standing behind a man. But this need not be the case. You can stand behind a person you believe in, or a cause, and be a leader as well. For example, when I stand behind my conviction that self-esteem is the most fundamental of all human rights, I become a spokesperson for what is so important to my heart. It's the same when I stand behind my commitment to people I love. I am not diminished by my position. On the contrary, I feel more of myself when I place that self in service to my commitments. I don't lose my freedom by standing behind my convictions, or by standing behind the people who are important to me. When I stand up for what I believe in, or whom I love, I make a stand for myself in this world. And where I stand on issues and principles helps to define me as a human being. Everyone stands for something in this life. And what you stand for is ultimately where you stand!

When I give sessions, I learn valuable lessons about lending support. Different therapists have different modes of working, which not only relate to the therapist/client relationship but can also be applied to all relationships. I try to support and be nonintrusive at the same time. I respect my client's space, process, choices, and responsibility for the work he does on himself. Different clients need different types of support. Often, it depends on their birth type. Even with the same client, the style of support will tend to vary from session to session. For example, one person needs a lot of coaching, talking, and physical support. Perhaps he was neglected as a child. Perhaps he didn't attach to his mother at birth. Maybe he was unwanted. Another needs to be reassured with affirmations and acknowledgments. Perhaps he suffers from low self-esteem. Maybe his father disapproved of him constantly. A third needs to be supported in feeling his feelings. Perhaps he was not allowed to cry as a child. Maybe he came from a family where he had to justify every little feeling and finally decided it was easier not to feel. Maybe he's an incest survivor. Another was physically abused and any touching triggers a violent reaction. My basic rule is that giving people time and space is essential, but some more than others need that time and space filled up with active support.

In extending support, please remember these guidelines. Don't lend it, then ask for it back. Giving in order to obligate someone to give back to you is not really giving at all. Also, don't offer support from a condescending position. In other words, don't feel sorry for someone, think you are superior, and look down at the person you're helping. I remind you that the one you are supporting is your equal, and your soul is vitally connected to his. Finally, don't lend support to prove your own worthiness. Your essence is your real worth. Who you are is good enough. When you are just being yourself, your heart radiates a healing energy that is the ultimate support. It's not all your doing but all your *being* that matters the most. Having said that, please don't just sit and meditate and think that's always enough. Once you know your intrinsic value, you can stop sitting and start taking action.

The path of extended support is one of the greatest journeys of love and compassion. Ironically, when you give for the sheer joy of giving, your gifts surely come back to you multiplied and when you least expect it. Moreover, if you truly give support freely, you receive instant gratification.

The Pitfall

The *pitfall* on the path to support is caretaking, rescuing, controlling, and manipulating. If you are lacking self-esteem and supporting others to obligate them to love you, you are making a sad mistake in relationships. You are worthy of love because of who you are, not what you do. You don't have to earn love by taking care of others, rehabilitating them, fixing them, and expecting their love in return. Rather, you want to extend support because it increases your awareness of your self as an interconnected member of the human family. Giving support freely is a reward in itself. Offering a helping hand strengthens you as well as the one who needs help. Beware of the temptation to form unhealthy, codependent relationships. While everyone needs support once in a while, if the foundation of your relationship is rescue, the structure you are building is based on weakness not strength. So, yes, extend support. It renders you more whole. But always remember that the one you are supporting is your equal, and that you are receiving equal value in the process.

Steps on the Fourth Journey

1. Extend support for the pleasure of it.
2. Feel how deeply you care about people.
3. Ask others how they would like to be supported.
4. Pray for those you love.
5. Be sensitive when people don't want your support.
6. Learn the difference between caretaking and caregiving.
7. Notice when support feels like sacrifice.
8. Stand up for what you believe in, and whom you love.
9. Your helping hand helps you.
10. Respect the dignity of those you support.
11. Do good deeds because they make you feel good indeed.

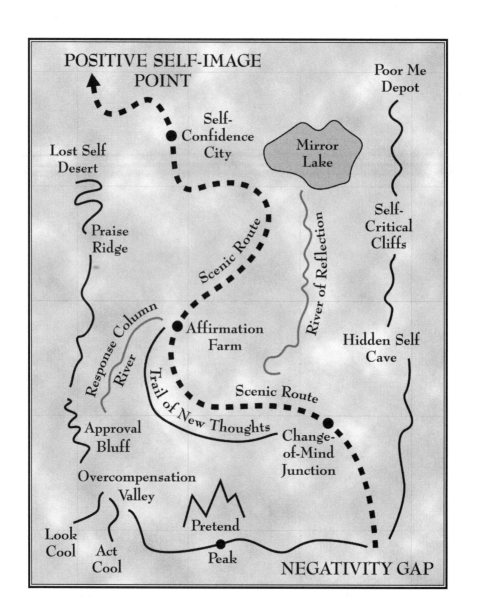

Journey 5

The Scenic Route to
a Positive Self-Image

As you journey, your mind can wander. It can soar to the highest peaks or sink to the lowest valleys. When your mind drifts, any thought can enter, and often you feel you can't do anything about it. Fortunately, you can. You have the power to think what you want and discard the rest, and depending on how you employ this power, your image of yourself will be either positive or negative.

You are not your thoughts about yourself. You are the thinker of those thoughts, the space in which those thoughts occur. Nevertheless, your experience of yourself is often determined by the quality of the thoughts, decisions, and beliefs you hold about yourself. Creating a positive self-image is taking responsibility for how you perceive yourself, and also editing your self-esteem script so that you are the producer, director, and leading actor of a positive, feel-good movie.

You have the power to look good and feel good as you journey to the center of yourself. Begin this part of your journey home by remembering that you are in the driver's seat, and that an optimistic self-image is a vehicle that can help deliver you to your destination.

◇ ◇ ◇ ◇ ◇ ◇ ◇ ◇ ◇ ◇

Pierre and Patricia have a beautiful son with very high self-esteem. They love to dress David in fashionable clothes, which are delightfully becoming on him. One day the three of them went strolling on the Champs-Elysées in Paris. They entered a boutique, and the salesperson looked at the two-year-old boy in the stroller and said, "My, what elegant trousers you have!" David looked down at his pants, lifted his feet in the air, and said, "And what about my shoes?"

A POSITIVE SELF-IMAGE

As you journey toward greater self-awareness and sacred ground, you notice that there are many circumstances you influence directly, others you affect indirectly, plus a multitude of things totally beyond your sphere of influence. You can surely control what you think of yourself and what you think of others. What others think of you is beyond your domain and pointless to worry about. Your self-esteem is a function of being the authority of your own life rather than needing external validation. Until you are number one in your own mind, you will always make yourself an understudy on life's stage and resent others for bathing in the limelight. So, the following journey leads you to the magical land where you can be a wizard, transforming your experience of yourself by changing the scenery of your own mind.

You take the scenic route out of Negativity Gap and head for Change of Mind Junction. Follow the trail of new thoughts to Affirmation Farm. Then head for Mirror Lake and Self-Confidence City. The scenery is outstanding. Just like you.

It happened at a workshop in New York City. I was going around the room checking on the participants. It was a relatively large group and people were paired up, facing their partners, alternately telling each other "I am important." For many people it was an exercise full of emotion. Assistants were handing out Kleenex. Some felt the excitement of the thought and began to shout it out passionately. Others felt held back by self-doubt and fear, bowing their heads in shame. I stopped in front of one woman who just could not get the words out. Whenever she tried, she fell into the malapropism, "I am impotent."

I looked at her name tag. Julie. I leaned over and whispered in her ear, "Important, Julie, not impotent," and she looked up at me. Her face scrunched up as though it was smashed against a window. "I can't say that," she said. I asked her why not. She replied that she didn't know but it wasn't true and she couldn't say it. I asked her how she knew it wasn't true, and she replied that the very idea of being important went against everything she was brought up to believe. Then her partner bent over and said to her, "Julie, you *are* important. Whether you believe it or not, you *are.*" Julie began sobbing, with her head in her lap.

Julie shared with the whole group after the exercise. "It was never okay for me to be important. My twin brother, sure. Jimmy was the one they wanted all along. He came out first. When they discovered I was there, my father's comment was, 'What's this—not a girl too?' I was like afterbirth or something. Jimmy was Daddy's trophy. My only use was to shadow him. When we were in preschool, I used to follow him like a puppy. Then, when we were older, I became his caretaker, his emotional rescue remedy. To this day he thinks all women were placed on this planet to wait on him."

Julie was unwanted as a woman and unwelcome in the world. She shared that she came from a long line of unwanted women. Her mother was one of three sisters, all unwanted. Her mother's mother was an only child, also unwanted as a woman. "It's my family tradition to be unwanted, unloved, and unimportant as a woman." Suddenly, the group started acknowledging her spontaneously all over again.

"You're such a beautiful woman."

"So elegant."

"So feminine."

"You're a remarkable woman."

"A very important woman." Julie shook her head. "Important? It's a new word for me. I never even felt like I existed before now."

AFFIRMATION FARM

You enter Affirmation Farm, where your new thoughts about yourself grow like seeds into sprouts into blossoms. Start with simple seeds like "I am important," "I'm number one," "I'm intelligent," "I'm good enough." Write each one twenty times a day, with a response column. You can also say them to yourself in front of a mirror, or make a tape of them. When you begin with this technique, it may seem silly, or you may resist it because it reminds you of repetitive writing assignments in school. As with any tool, it will only work if you use it. If you want a rich harvest, you must start with some healthy seeds.

It is spiritually trendy these days to think that "thought is creative and you are the thinker." It's fairly obvious. You first have to conceive of something before you actually create it. If you want to build a house, first you need to picture it in your mind. You need a blueprint. If you want to write a book, first you need to have the idea. And if you want to raise your self-esteem, you begin with an idea, the inspiration.

There is a deeper meaning to the philosophy of creative thought that warrants our attention. There is the idea of *the power of positive thinking*, the belief that thinking something makes it true. This philosophy encompasses a whole range of techniques, including affirmations, subliminal learning, and hypnotic suggestion. The notion that you create your reality with your mind usually includes the fact that most of what we think is unconscious. The conscious mind is simply the tip of the iceberg. Your thoughts are constantly attracting, projecting, and creating results, but most of the results you experience are the product of your subconscious, or unconscious, mind. According to this line of reasoning, if your conscious mind is thinking "I create wealth" and your result is poverty, there must be some deeper, unconscious negative factor blocking the flow of money. Therefore, if you analyze your unconscious mind, discover the limiting thought, change it into an affirmation, and write the new positive thought twenty times a day for a few weeks, your financial situation should show a dramatic improvement. Or you can simply get a subliminal tape on prosperity and submerge your subconscious mind in a sea of rich thoughts. That's the theory.

I think it is only partially true. If it were completely true, many struggling people I know would be millionaires, many lonely people happily married, and many sick people miraculously healed. There is certainly more to creation than the human mind. You could, for example, affirm for a hundred years that winters in Moscow are hot, but the chances are it will still be snowing there January 1, 2100 (although with global warming you never know). You could listen to a subliminal tape affirming that you are six inches taller, fifty pounds lighter, and your eyes a different color, and probably nothing will change. Furthermore, you could affirm that everyone you meet falls in love with you and gives you all their money and, in all likelihood, your results would not correspond to your thoughts.

What do you create? What *don't* you create? How can you avoid confusion on this topic and maintain your metaphysical boundaries as well as your common sense? To begin with, you don't create external reality. Creation is unfolding continuously and you are a part of that unfolding, but not the sole source of it. You also don't create other people's behavior toward you. If someone is abusing you, you don't create his abusive actions. You may journey toward such behavior if you have a history of abuse in your family. You certainly create and are responsible for your response to that abuse. But you don't create what other people do. It is very important to know this. You are not responsible for others.

You might, however, have grown up believing you are responsible for others. You may have inherited guilt. Your mother says to you, "You're making your father angry." You feel your culpability. Your father says to you, "You're driving your mother crazy." You feel delusions of grandeur. None of it was true. You never made anyone feel anything. Nobody ever made you feel anything. You did what you did and your mother, father, brothers, and sisters had their response to it. However, if you never recovered from your family tradition of false responsibility, you can be carrying the burden without even knowing it. You can, for instance, begin to affirm that your husband no longer drinks, your wife no longer complains, and your business partners all look up to you . . . with no results. Why? Your sphere of influence does not extend to those people. You have simply projected onto your adult reality a fantasy you took on as a child. This type of transference often results in people's being in a state of "wishful thinking." It's like affirming "Someday my prince will come." Maybe he will, maybe he won't. And if he does come, maybe he'll truly be a princely prince, or just a frog.

◇ ◇ ◇ ◇

I remember bringing the International Self-Esteem Seminar to Lyon, France. On Sunday morning I invited the participants to come up front and shout, "I'm number one!" stomping a foot to punctuate the point. The exercise was voluntary, but many people took advantage of the opportunity. As the exercise went on, I noticed a lady in the back of the room whose arm kept going up and down whenever I asked for another volunteer. Finally, I caught her with her arm up and she slowly moved toward the front of the room. Nora was painfully shy. She bowed her head and took tiny steps, prolonging the time it would take to reach me. As soon as she tried to face the group, she flushed bright pink and asked if she could sit down. I encouraged her first to tell everyone she was number one. The group cheered her on.

Nora just couldn't do it. The words would catch in her throat. Her foot could not stomp. She had no authority in her body language. The group raised its level of support. Nora wanted to crawl into a hole. She kept smiling and apologizing, offering to sit down. "I'm taking up too much time," she whispered to me. "It's okay," I replied. "You're number one. People love it when you take up their time." She shook her head. "I'm number one?" "It's not a question, it's an answer," I said. She giggled. I asked her to look up, not down. She proceeded to look up at the ceiling. I straightened her head so that she was facing the group. "Oh, my God, there are so many of them." Everyone laughed kindly. "Yes," I replied, "but you're number one."

Nora decided to give it a good try. She was saying the words now. "I AM number one. I AM number one." The only problem was it sounded as though she was trying to convince herself, rather than express a true conviction. Furthermore, when she attempted to put her foot down and say the words at the same time, it looked like she was afraid she would hurt the carpet. I asked her whom she was trying to convince and she immediately replied, "My father." Her entire demeanor began to shift as the realization swept through her body. "He would never let me be number one. NEVER." Her voice was growing stronger. "I was the third born. My brother came first, so of course he was number one." She spontaneously waved a fist at him. "Then came my sister. She was the number-one girl. Couldn't do anything wrong." The other fist waved at her. "I was an accident, I'm certain. A mistake. I was conceived by a hole in his condom. The BASTARD! He never even acknowledged my presence." She shook both fists at him. "I remember telling him once that I had won a spelling bee at school. I thought he'd be so proud. He just looked past me as if I didn't exist, as if I wasn't even there, and asked my mother when dinner would be ready. I never opened my heart to him, or any man, after that. NEVER!" A chill swept the room. "I'M NUMBER ONE," she screamed at the top of her lungs. Stomping her foot like thunder, she cried, "I'M NUMBER ONE, GODDAMNIT!" The room went wild in agreement with Nora's new thought.

◊ ◊ ◊ ◊

Your sphere of influence does extend throughout one important kingdom of your life, however. Your thoughts create your experience. They define the way you perceive your world and, most importantly, yourself. Thus, if you want to journey to greater self-love, it is essential that you paint a positive picture of yourself.

Thinking good, loving thoughts about yourself is as natural as loving a baby. Or a parent. You are lovable. You are as wonderful and innocent as the child you were the day you were born. It's true. All of creation is awesome and you are a part of the divine scheme of things. Affirming your own beauty, intelligence, power, goodness, and innocence is simply a way of reminding yourself of the truth. Why do you walk around with that internal courtroom in eternal session, judging yourself as bad, wrong, stupid, ugly, weak, and guilty? In my opinion, it is a form of blasphemy to use the words "I am," which is one biblical translation of God's name, in conjunction with a lot of negativity. Nevertheless, most people see it the other way around. They think that their negativity is their humility and that having too much self-confidence is prideful, arrogant, and egotistical.

I was brought up never to show off. Moreover, I was subtly told that I should not stand out too much. After all, I was Jewish, and if we Jews get too uppity, the Nazis cart us off to the gas chambers. I wasn't told these exact words, but the message was implied often enough. I remember once being told, "If you stand out in a crowd, people might notice you." So? I could never figure that one out. It seemed like some impossible riddle. Once, when I was at that stage of being obsessed with winning, my mother warned me, "Be careful. Sometimes, it's better to finish second than first." Or she would say, "Don't call attention to yourself. Let others have the light."

❖ ❖ ❖ ❖

Mallie was playing with our grandsons, Sammy and Jake. Sammy burst out, "You know, Gammy, I'm the smartest one in my class." Mallie became quiet, not wanting to diminish Sammy's sense of himself but also wanting to teach him a lesson in equality. Then she said, "That's great, Sammy. And who's the funniest person in your class?" He thought for a moment and then responded, "Tommy's the funniest." "And who's the best listener?" "Hmmm. That would be Sally." "The best singer?" "The best athlete?" As Sammy answered, he was getting to see, yes, he might be the smartest, but everyone else was the best at something too.

❖ ❖ ❖ ❖

When you toot your own horn, it does not have to be from a position of superiority. You are simply taking your place in the orchestra of humanity. You are great. You are important. You are even magnificent and so is everyone else. When you remember to balance your improving opinion of yourself with the realization that others are your equal, you can give up the guilt of being as extraordinary as you are. Everyone is extraordinary.

It's ordinary to be extraordinary. There is no point in subordinating yourself in your own mind out of your consideration for others. That only renders them superior, transferring your guilt to them. We are all equally innocent and magical. Just get used to the idea. Or, as my granddaughter Ariana says, "Just deal with it!"

Parents often don't want to spoil their children with praise, and it is true that the most valuable acknowledgment you can give a child is the ability to validate herself. The problem is, however, if a child gets the message that tooting her own horn implies she is spoiled, she might do the opposite, repressing her self-esteem for fear that it looks like she is spoiled or insensitive to others.

Another problem arises when parents can't say no to a child. While it is important to say yes to the soul of a child and teach him to say yes to himself, it is equally valuable to say no when a no is called for. If a parent cannot give his developing child a healthy sense of boundaries, the child never develops those internal boundaries that help to define a realistic sense of the world surrounding him. Often, the parent who cannot say no was the child whose parents never said yes. It can, however, be the other way around. If you always heard no as a kid, you might grow into an adult who just doesn't know how to say yes.

Everyone loved Courtney. She stood out in the group, a shining star. At first she basked in the attention, participated in all the group exercises, and enjoyed receiving the acknowledgment she attracted. But when I asked volunteers to stand in front of the room and proclaim, "I stand out in a crowd!," even though there was no pressure, Courtney spontaneously began to diminish in size. She curled into a ball and hid herself under her chair. The process continued with only the people around her noticing what was happening. Then, the whole room was drawn into the drama.

Courtney was breathing deeply and crying and shouting for people to leave her alone. Everyone wanted to give her more support but, in her case, physical proximity was the opposite of support. Slowly, I approached her. I kneeled to her level and caught her eye. She told me not to come closer and I nodded. We established a safe distance. I just stayed with her like that for several minutes. Finally, she whispered, "I don't want to stand out in a crowd." I said that was okay, she didn't have to. "I want to hide." I encouraged her to relax, nobody was going to force her to be seen. She proceeded to recite a litany of negative thoughts, continuing to breathe and release them. "I have to be invisible." "I'm bad." "I'm an intrusion." "I don't deserve to be here." "I should be dead." "I'm always wrong." "I'm a troublemaker." "I'm sorry I'm taking up all this time." "I'm so sorry." And finally she wailed from a place deep in her soul.

I approached closer and gently stroked her head. I assured her that she was doing great. She wasn't taking up any more of our time than we were of her time. She looked up at me, more present now. She smiled. She laughed. "I deserve to be here, don't I?" "You surely do," I replied. "Wow," she said, just "wow."

Later, Courtney explained that when she was in the womb, her mother had hidden the pregnancy, and in many ways, Courtney had been hiding all her life. When I had asked her to say she stood out in a crowd, she simply couldn't. "Hey, Courtney," a friend of hers said. "You do stand out in a crowd. Even when you hide under a chair." We all laughed because it was so obviously true.

SELF-CONFIDENCE CITY

You enter this amazing city and immediately feel the difference. The boutiques are beautiful, the restaurants elegant, and the theaters all showing very upbeat movies about real people. The whole city is glittering, sparkling with electric energy. But what's most amazing of all is the quality of the people walking up and down the streets—good-looking, well-dressed, smiling people, obviously happy to be themselves. You get out of your car and take your place in Self-Confidence City. As you walk down the sidewalk, you can't help but saunter, feeling light and lovable. Your head is up and your chest is full. It's not that you're full of yourself or faking feeling good. It's more a genuine feeling of faith in yourself, knowing you're important, valuable, and powerful. You have this new attitude that you can do anything you set out to do. You have the sense of being a living "success story." All those affirmations are buzzing in the cells of your body. All those little seedlings have blossomed into a new you.

When you stand in front of a mirror, what do you see? Most people are very self-critical of their own appearance. I remember when I first met Mallie, she had a habit of badmouthing herself in front of a mirror. I suggested after a while that whenever she looked in the mirror she immediately tell herself three things she liked about what she saw. It's a matter of training your eyes to see what's beautiful, that's all. The more Mallie practiced this simple exercise, the more she came to appreciate her own beauty, a quality the world had noticed long before. After all, she had been a cover girl for the *Saturday Evening Post,* a well-known magazine some years ago.

Not that you are an image in a mirror. Not that you are only a body. We all know that beauty is not skin-deep. A beautiful soul can reside within any body. A model can have terrible self-hatred. And God knows the current obsession with having a perfect body, whatever "perfect" may be, can result in serious mental, emotional, and physical problems. Nevertheless, it is true that your body is the way you are seen by the world and by yourself. It is somewhat delusional to think you can have high self-esteem but cannot stand the sight of your own body. So begin by letting go of your judgments. Shift your thoughts about what is beautiful. Transcend your cultural prejudice about beauty, weight, height, hair color, eye color, whatever! And affirm your beauty to yourself. Hold your feet and talk to them about their strength, support, and innocence. Talk to your hands, your face, your neck, and your shoulders. Love your body.

We all have been brainwashed by advertising, movies, and videos to have a very narrow-minded definition of beauty. Teenagers become bulimic or anorexic to conform to an unhealthy notion of beauty. True beauty emanates from a state of wellness and divine inner light. It has nothing to do with the images projected by Hollywood and Madison Avenue.

The bottom line is that beauty is in the eye of the beholder. This pertains to the way you see beauty not only in others, but in yourself as well. So, when you look at yourself in the mirror, you the beholder of you the beholden have the opportunity to focus on your true beauty, or the ways in which you fall short in comparison to some phony image. Whatever you focus on will expand in your experience. The choice is yours. And you will live with the consequences of your choices.

I often suggest to my clients that they alter their appearance intentionally as a way to raise their self-esteem. One day dress up to the hilt. If you need to, buy a great new outfit and let yourself look splashy. The next day dress down, understate your presentation, and let yourself look sloppy. When you arrive at the point where you feel equally good about yourself no matter what you are wearing, then you know you have a deep sense of self-worth.

It's so important to know you are really a treasure. Nowadays, people wear designer labels like badges of prestige. Nike, Air Jordan, Calvin Klein, Hugo Boss, Polo—as though these visible images adorning your body can somehow create real self-esteem. I think it's very sad when you need someone else's name on your clothes to feel good about yourself. Try wearing a shirt with your own name on it.

My grandson Jake paints a very positive picture of himself. One day, when he was three, he said to me: "Gampy, when I grow up, I'm going to be just like you." "Really?" "Yes. And when you grow up, you're going to be just like me." "No kidding, Jake." Then, after thinking about it, I added, "Exactly what do you mean by that, Jake?" "It's simple, Gampy. When I grow up I'm gonna be just as big as you, and when you grow up you're going to be just as smart as me!"

The Pitfall

The *pitfall* en route to a positive self-image is to believe that you are no more than your thoughts about yourself. You can very easily reduce yourself to a positive-thinking machine, an automaton that has brainwashed itself to repeat positive thoughts endlessly, unaware of all other aspects of its being. You can, if you wish, live life entirely in your head, your mind, your ego, having successfully replaced your negative self-image with a positive one. If you disassociated as a child in trauma, retreating to fantasies in your mind, you can use your positive self-image to simply induce more fantasy. You can be disconnected from your emotional body, still terrified to feel the real pain that caused you to escape in the first place. The result is that you become an *upwardly displaced person,* as though you have vacated your body and headed for the high hills of your mind. If you find yourself tumbling into this pitfall, it is time to give your mind a sorely needed rest. Pay more attention to your heart, your feelings, and your body. Do physical work on yourself. Receive a massage. Use your hands. Work in a garden. Wash your car by hand. Do the laundry. Look at someone you love and breathe deeply. Go to an emotional movie and feel what you feel. Find a therapist who can redirect you to your emotional life. You deserve a healthy heart as well as a healthy mind!

Steps on the Fifth Journey

1. You are number one in your life.
2. Your mind is a powerful tool. Use it.
3. Let go of your negative thoughts.
4. You are important.
5. You are intelligent.
6. Think of yourself as a "success story."
7. Look in the mirror and focus on your beauty.
8. Talk to yourself in a positive voice.
9. Give yourself pep talks when necessary.
10. Develop an attitude of "Thank God I'm me!"
11. Have an attitude of confidence. You *can* do it.

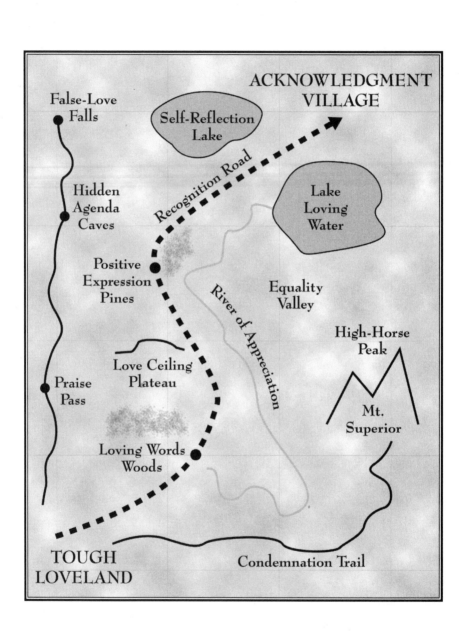

Journey 6

The Road of Recognition

The power of recognition should not be underestimated. Both for the giver and the receiver, the energy exchanged in the honest display of public or private appreciation is healing, enlivening, and uplifting. Since love can elicit the entire gamut of emotions, the receiving of acknowledgment can wash away old wounds and replace them with a buzz of excitement. While it may provide only a temporary hit unless it can attach itself to an internal sense of worthiness, recognition can also reflect genuine self-esteem and even expand it.

When you take the road of recognition, your journey home is accelerated. Those you acknowledge become the guides, the beacons, the light that shows you the way. You can recognize people for a wide variety of gifts, both internal and external— their intelligence, humor, honesty, loyalty, kindness, sensitivity, creativity, innocence, and beauty. Or their support, assistance, cooperation, feedback, lessons, and good work. It might feel awkward at first, especially if you have a lifetime habit of being reserved and withholding compliments. Perhaps you think praise sounds false. But there is a difference between false praise, which usually carries a hidden agenda, and the spontaneous expression of genuine appreciation, which springs from a well deep in your core that needs to shower others with love.

When you lavish recognition on others, endorphins are released in your bloodstream, circulating healthy, loving energy from your head to your toes. The cells of your body smile in unison.

Traveling on Recognition Road is a reflective journey. What you recognize in others is a mirror of your inner qualities. If you give acknowledgment to someone who cannot receive it, it is still worth your while. Perhaps you will need to adjust your language a little, because everyone hears things differently. But if you make it your mission to remind all the important people in your life just how important they are, your journey home will be full of self-awakening and happy memories.

I was working with a class of thirty kids, all eight years old. We were playing a self-esteem game. After each child took his or her turn in front of the room, the class trying to guess his or her secret good quality, I asked them all a question. "Did any of you happen to notice how you all looked while you were trying to guess the of her secret qualities?" "Funny?" asked Jessica, who seemed to need to go first all the time. "Weird?" joked William, clearly the class clown. "Not at all," I said. "When you were saying good things about each other, you looked beautiful. You actually light up when you express love to someone else." "Really?" asked a girl named Debby. "Really," I responded. "I'll show you."

I asked Debby to stand in front of the group and everyone else to say what they liked about her. I also told them they should look at the person giving the compliment, not at Debby. One by one they shouted out her wonderful qualities. She was smart, a good singer, a good friend, pretty (lots of giggles), and kind. After a minute or two, I stopped them, and asked if they could see it. "I saw it," said Jessica. "Everyone's eyes get full of light when they say nice things." "Yeah," added William. "Kind of like E. T." One by one, they admitted they could see it. Then William turned to the teacher, Mrs. Matthews. "Mrs. Matthews, you're the best teacher in the whole world." While Mrs. Matthews blushed, William beamed. "Look at William," Jessica said. "He's all lit up."

THE ROAD OF RECOGNITION

The power of recognition has been well researched, documented, and reported, but usually from the point of view of the benefits to the one receiving the verbal affection. And while I don't deny these benefits, I balance them against the more lasting strength that self-validation provides. As I have suggested previously, praising a child can be counterproductive if it leads to a kind of Pavlovian response. Many children grow up addicted to the need for praise, which further distances them from their inner selves. Having said this, the power of recognition is undeniable, both to the giver and recipient. For the recipient it can produce emotional healing. For the giver it comes as a blessing.

Take a walk up Recognition Road. Leaving Tough Loveland, head for Loving Words Woods and the River of Appreciation. Move on to Positive Expression Pines and Lake Loving Water. When you arrive at Acknowledgment Village you can reflect on the many wonderful qualities you possess that you can now see in others.

Training your mind to be an acknowledging partner instead of a critical parent can be a challenge, but it is a task well worth the undertaking. If you begin as I suggested in Journey 5 by acknowledging yourself frequently, both by writing affirmations and saying them aloud in front of a mirror, it should become easier to extend this positive outlook toward others. Developing an affirmative attitude can start with little things. When you are on an airplane or train, look at the people around you and think positive thoughts about them. Or do this even walking down the street or at the office. *Allow a minor acquaintance to become a major opportunity.* Notice when your mind tends to be tempted by judgment. Do you rush to judge when you are in a new situation and feel afraid of being judged yourself? Is it a form of self-defense? Attack first? Preemptive first strike? When you find yourself doing this, say "Excuse me" to that internal judge and shift your focus from your mind to your heart. You can always think of something nice to think and say about someone, no matter how unimportant it may seem to you. There is no such thing as insignificant acknowledgment. *Love is never trivial.*

It's a good idea to begin and end each day with recognition of yourself and others. When you first see your mate, your children, or your colleagues, begin your first conversation of the day with each one of them on a positive note. Acknowledge them. And try to do the same thing the last time you communicate with people every day. In the Bible we are told, "Never let the sun set on your anger." Complete each day with love in your heart—with mercy, clemency, and forgiveness when possible. That way you won't wake up the next morning with prior evidence for your interior judge. Your innocence will be restored.

Become accustomed to speaking sentences that begin with the following phrases:

"Something I really like about you is ___."

"Something I really appreciate about you is ___."

"Something terrific about you is ___."

"Something I cherish about you is ___."

"Something wonderful about you is ___."

"Something I acknowledge you for is ___."

"Something I'm grateful to you for is ___."

"Something truly unique about you is ___."

"Something I will never forget about you is ___."

"Something I recognize in you is ___."

◇ ◇ ◇ ◇

Mallie and I were conducting a Couples Retreat on the island of Mykonos in the beautiful Aegean Sea. We had a small group of couples, mostly from Italy. One couple, Antonio and Sylvia, were older than the rest, retired and looking to begin a new life together. They were quite beautiful physically, but very traditional in their ways. He had decided that, after a corporate career, he wanted to be a gentleman farmer, and she was a very elegant lady. At one point, we were sharing about beginning every day in the tub together, acknowledging each other and communicating what was on our minds, be it the dreams of the night before or the goals of the day to come. We could see Antonio and Sylvia giggle as they went off. The next morning we all got together to share. After everyone had a turn, Sylvia, who seemed to have a new glow, said that she had something significant to share. She reported that for the first time ever in their relationship, she and Antonio had taken a shower together and expressed their love for each other under the falling water. Mallie looked at me and waved for a tissue.

LOVING WORDS WOODS

A sign greets you as you enter these woods: "Think loving thoughts in these woods. Speak loving words." The woods are tall redwoods, hundreds of years old. As you walk through them, you imagine all the loving thoughts and words they have heard in their lifetime. It is a magnificent woods and you are filled with emotion. You sit on a stone and gather your thoughts. Your mind is suddenly flooded with loving thoughts about the many people you have known and loved in your life. As you walk on, you meet an occasional traveler—one an old friend, another a stranger, and then a family member. To each you offer spontaneous words of love, recognition of something wonderful you see in him or her. Walking quietly out of the woods, you reflect on yourself and the fullness of love you carry in your heart.

Often, people have a difficult time receiving recognition. If your self-esteem is low, you will not want to hear other people's good thoughts about you. You will turn away, withdraw, think they are lying, or deflect the conversation. Here are some typical examples I have witnessed.

Dylan: "I really like your haircut, Zoe."
Zoe: "I hate it. It makes my face fat."

Natasha: "You look really great, Lucy."
Lucy: "Are you talking to me?"

Tyrone: "Great tie, Billy."
Billy: "Five dollars at Kmart."

Graciela: "You are such a wonderful human being."
Marcus: "I thought we'd go for pizza."

Justin: "You cook one amazing lasagna, Maya."
Maya: "It's my mother's recipe."

Sam: "You are so gorgeous, Sophie!"
Sophie: "Wait till you meet my sister."

We've all experienced it. Someone, in all sincerity, tells us something wonderful about ourselves. We turn away, blush, change the subject, or deny it outright. Why is it that when someone criticizes you, you take it to heart, make it an ordeal, and believe it is true while when you are praised you can't fathom that what's being said might actually be true? It's your addiction to disapproval, that's all. You are convinced that the judge knows what he's talking about and his word is the last judgment! You think he is God! Then when someone tells you the honest, loving truth about yourself, you're sure he's a godforsaken liar.

Rubbish!

If you knew yourself as indeed you are, a vital part of the miracle of creation, you would never again be able to pretend you were less than amazing. You would realize how normal and right it is to be loved. You would give up the struggle to earn love and know that you are already worthy. Moreover, you would let go of your guilt and stop thinking that when you receive love, there's less for someone else. There *is* no scarcity of love. Love is a self-replenishing, life-affirming energy. Love wants to grow. Love is quantum. Get with the program. When someone offers you recognition, smile and say thank you. No other response is required.

In any language, the most powerful words of acknowledgment are "I love you." These three words are what we are born to hear, learn, and pass along. An old song goes, "Love ain't nothing till you give it away." Love cannot be contained, possessed, or owned. It must be passed on. It must move. It is more like a river than a piece of property. And self-love is no different. You feel the love in you, then you touch someone else with that love. When you touch someone else with your love, it awakens her love so she can pass it on. In this way, love can gather momentum as we share it.

Listen to the wonderful song by Stevie Wonder called "These Three Words."

"I love you." These words have many meanings, but all the meanings have elements in common: Compassion. Connection. Contact. I feel for you. I care for you. I love you. Sometimes love is spiritual. I love God. I love the sacred. Sometimes love is mental. I love humanity. I love the planet. Love can also be a deep heart-connection among friends. Love can be sexual. And love can be the glue that binds a family together. In any case, love is chemistry. When you open your heart, a chemical process occurs in your brain and throughout your body. Oxytocin, "the love hormone," is emitted. Endorphins flood your bloodstream. A sense of bliss overtakes you. You get high.

❖ ❖ ❖ ❖

Jasmine was so embarrassed when her partner was telling her "I love you," I thought she'd fall off her seat. Instead, she squirmed, arms crossed, twisted torso, and pulled at her hair vigorously. She was at one of our annual Valentine's Weekend Seminars here in Connecticut. She talked, laughed, cried, and did everything possible to change the words, obstruct the flow of energy, and get out of the line of fire.

Later, she shared her story. She never remembered her mom saying, "I love you." She knew her mother loved her. It was just not her way to use those words. Instead, her mom would say, "God bless you!" Jasmine grew up with an abundance of God's blessings, but never did she hear the words she wanted to hear. Even as an adult, she would be leaving her mom's house, or completing a telephone conversation, and she would say, "I love you, Mom." The response would be the same. "God bless you, dear." Finally, one day, Jasmine had had enough of this. She was leaving her mother's home and her mom said the "God" words, whereupon Jasmine started crying and telling her mom what she wanted to hear. She made it perfectly clear that while "God bless you" are wonderful words, she had been waiting all her life for her mom to say, "I love you." Her mother was taken aback, but heard her daughter and said she would try.

Subsequently, whenever they talked on the phone, Jasmine would complete the conversation by saying, "I love you, Mom." Then there would be a pause, after which her mother would reply, "I love you too." Recently, Jasmine said, there had been even a deeper breakthrough. Now her mom was saying, "I love you" first, without any prompting.

But still she had trouble receiving these words from anyone other than her mother.

❖ ❖ ❖ ❖

Tell the people you love that you love them. Frequently. Tell your children, your parents, your mate, your friends, your family. Make it a point. Whenever I am on the telephone with someone I love, I always try to remember to complete the conversation with these three words. Also, when I am in someone's presence. Even if I am upset with the person, I try to leave them with my words of love. I want them to remember me by my love, not the other stuff.

There is an old myth that you should not use these words too frequently, but save them for special occasions. Nonsense. Every moment is a special occasion. You can lose a loved one in a flash. You never know if you will be afforded another opportunity to express your love. Don't postpone these important words. And don't mistake their meaning. "I love you" does not have to mean "I am in love with you" or "I want to make love with you." These three words are complete in themselves.

Love is the solution to so many problems. Expressing love spreads healing. Don't hold back. *When given the opportunity, speak the magic words.*

❖ ❖ ❖ ❖

Antonio was standing in front of a hundred people who were spontaneously standing up one by one and showering him with recognition.

"You're great, Antonio."

"You are so kind."

"Antonio, you're a great friend."

"I love the sound of your voice, Antonio."

"I love your eyes."

"I love you, Antonio." While Antonio was taking it in as best he could, a smile on his face fighting his tears, the group began to whisper in unison, "We love you, Antonio . . . we love you, Antonio. . . ."

Afterward, Antonio shared that in those moments he felt his body as pure energy, like a river of molecules. People in the group shared that they had felt the exact same way. Giving or receiving, you bathe in the same waters. Lake Loving Water.

ACKNOWLEDGMENT VILLAGE

Make this day a day of random acts of recognition. Wherever you go, whomever you contact, acknowledge that person. Be it your family, friends on the phone, neighbors, the mail carrier, the checkout lady in the supermarket, think of something really sweet to say about each person. If you go to work, offer recognition to the people you work with, even your boss. If you're stuck in traffic, silently acknowledge the drivers of the cars around you. If you're walking down the street, smile and make eye contact with as many people as possible, thinking of something nice about each one. And when you go to bed at night, close your eyes and acknowledge anyone else you might have missed during the day. Life is good in Acknowledgment Village.

In my mind, it is a natural and unchangeable law of nature that a parent love a child. While I recognize that there are some seriously disturbed adults having children these days, I believe that the large majority of human beings love their children, want to pick them up when they cry, and enjoy telling them how wonderful they are and how much they love them. This is normal. Nature's way.

An entire generation of doctors and psychologists, though, advised against nature for quite some time. Even Dr. Spock confessed he began his teaching with this incorrect paradigm. When DNA was discovered in 1953, it seemed to nail the lid on the coffin of a warm, loving environment being significant to the development of a child. The result of all this misinformation was a generation of parents who did not trust their own instincts to hold love in their hearts and express it to their children. Consequently, these children grew up in a cold, gray world, filled with world wars, cold wars, atomic weapons, terrorism, and environmental waste. By the time they reached adulthood, this cold, gray world appeared normal to them. It was the only world they knew, and they went to sleep every night thinking it was the only world there was. A world of cold, gray love.

Wrong. Cold love is no love, unjustifiable in any form.

Love is contagious health. This is why you should share these three words, "I love you," with your children frequently. It's good for them. It's good for *you.* If you don't tell them you love them, they don't hear these words where they most need to hear them: at home. Then, when they grow up, they find it difficult to tell their own children these words. It's your job to be a pioneer in your own family tradition. Repeat after me: "I love you." Say it frequently.

◇ ◇ ◇ ◇

Many of us grow up with a *love ceiling.* If our parents have not expressed love for us, if they have been cold, if they have shown too much "tough love" and not enough "tender love," the result is that we freeze when we are exposed to true love, and we tend to be blocked in our own ability to express the warmth of love. In reality, we froze as children for lack of warm love. But the frozen soul is felt by the adult who is confronted with hot love. You want to melt down, but your cellular memories cry no. You push away the very love that would heal you of your pain. When you become aware that you've hit your ceiling, take a breath and let more love touch you. Don't worry, you won't go through the roof.

You can feel as if you're out of control when someone is expressing love for you. It appears as though the giver is in control and the recipient is at the mercy of the donor. The truth, however, is that such thinking is a projection of your mind. When someone says they love you, that does not mean they want to control, obligate, or manipulate you. If you know you deserve the love, you can freely receive it. If you believe you are unworthy, then you feel indebted to the giver and think there will be payback time.

The truth is, when you afford someone the opportunity to shower you with love, you give the giver a great gift. And the giver is expanded by your ability to receive.

Listen to James Taylor singing "Shower the People You Love with Love." Let it motivate you to share words of love. Take a walk through Positive Expression Pines and express your loving thoughts from the bottom of your heart and the seat of your soul. Share them for the joy that is awakened in your heart as you utter them. The benefit you receive will be enhanced by the blessing you bestow on the one you love. On the other hand, if you veer off to Praise Pass or Hidden Agenda Caves, praising someone to oblige him to return the favor or, even worse, to bind him to you in some invisible way forever, forget it. Get back on Recognition Road. Let go of thinking that you can trick someone into taking you out of your solitude. Nobody but you can fill up the emptiness within you.

Many years ago Mallie and I were facilitating a workshop in Washington, D.C. The group was unusual in that there were several deaf people attending, and we had someone signing for them. They could read lips as well. As the seminar proceeded it became clear that these people who could not hear had each suffered some trauma concerning something forbidden that they had overheard, something terrible that had been said to them, or something important that they had not heard. Of course, they all had suffered physiological damage as well. In fact, they were functioning quite well with their handicaps. They hadn't come to the seminar for physical healing, but, rather, for open-heart therapy, which is what I do.

At one point during the training the group was paired up, doing a one-on-one acknowledgment process. I was observing two of the deaf women signing their love for each other. It was very moving to witness this silent exchange of loving feelings. One of the girls, Wanda, was glowing as she expressed her love for her friend Diane, who on the other hand seemed to be having a hard time receiving even silent love. I approached Diane and stood where she could see me, but her eyes avoided mine. I kneeled down to her eye level and asked her to take a deep breath. She immediately burst into tears.

Wanda was whispering the words "I love you" over and over in Diane's ears. First one ear, then the other. There was no lip-reading, no signing. Diane was breathing, feeling the energy, taking in the warm love that was so clearly radiating from Wanda's heart. The two friends were connected in some unseen exchange of spirit and heart. The exercise continued for a long time and the entire room was enveloped in loving emotion. When it was over, people were sharing about their experience. Finally, it was Diane's turn. What she signed was that Wanda's expression of love was so strong that she seemed to hear the actual words, "I love you."

You are never too young or too old to say "I love you." And never too deaf to hear words of love.

The Pitfall

The *pitfall* here is lack of balance. You can become a recognition junkie, forgetting to temper acknowledgment with better judgment. By "better judgment," I don't necessarily mean you should acknowledge people some of the time and judge them the rest of the time. What I am suggesting is that acknowledgment doesn't preclude the value of giving people some healthy feedback, or constructive criticism. Don't withhold your feedback because you think you should always be saying nice things to people. That's not the point. You want to be honest first, positive second, and supportive always.

Sometimes it is more supportive to share the flaws you observe in a person's behavior rather than just be on automatic pilot and praise him without thinking. You want to avoid being in denial of what is staring you in the face simply because you think you should always be positive. Yes, be a positive person, but be honest and loving first. Just as when you are really loving yourself, you are motivated to improve yourself to be all you can be, so it is with others. When you really love someone, you care about him, and therefore you summon the courage to tell him the truth. When you see something he might need to learn to improve his life, you are willing to share your perception.

Phrasing is important when giving feedback. Make sure you are not attacking with your energy. And always ask the person for permission to give feedback before you begin. "Would you like me to give you some feedback on this situation?" Don't be a space invader. Once you receive permission, begin with acknowledgment, such as "I really think you are an amazing person. . . ." Always launch your feedback with loving energy. And avoid the word "but," because it implies conditions. Instead, say something like this: "I really think you are an amazing person and there's this one little thing about you that doesn't make sense. Why do you always change the subject when I tell you how much I love you?"

Steps on the Sixth Journey

1. Think of good things to say to people.
2. Tell everyone in your family what you like about them.
3. Learn the language of love and the art of positive self-expression.
4. Feel the joy of telling someone how wonderful she is.
5. Practice random acts of recognition.
6. Be generous in spirit as well as in deed.
7. Surpass yourself with expressions of appreciation.
8. Recognize the accomplishments of others.
9. Shower your children with verbal appreciation.
10. Never hold back a heartfelt compliment.
11. Get high on loving words.

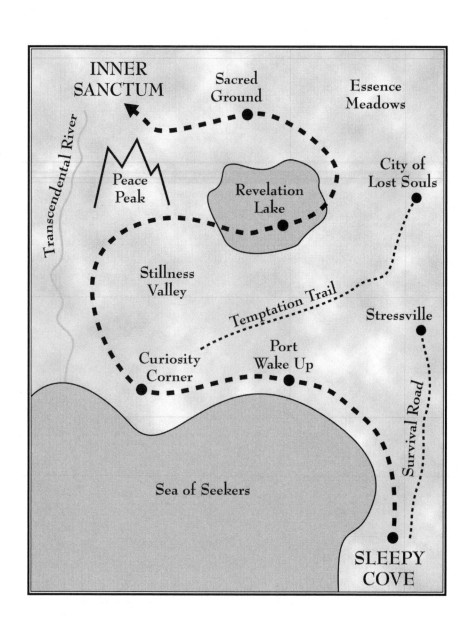

Journey 7

The Search for Inner Sanctum

Life is sacred, and you're alive. There is no denying the fact that you are a part of divine Creation. Whether you call it God, Spirit, Universal Force, or Cosmic Direction, an Unseen Intelligence seems to guide our lives and the flow of the universe. Either that or an amazing confluence of accidents. In either case life is a magical mystery we are all a part of.

As you go through your daily activities, it is easy to lose your connection to the miraculous. Life can become robotic and you can sleepwalk from one event to another, numb to the wonder and awe of it all. You might drift through your life like a leaf on a stream, forgetting both the tree you fell from and the heavens that feed the stream. You might be prime for a spiritual awakening.

As beauty is in the eye of the beholder, miracles are a reflection of an awakened soul. But how do you awaken to your own soul and therefore to the wonder of Creation? There are many ways, and surely you have your own. The important thing is not the specific path, but rather that you not neglect this vital journey. The return home to yourself is more than a mental bridge you cross, a healing of past pain, and simple self-esteem. It is as well a spiritual act, a process of self-realization, the recognition of Inner Light, and the revelation of Inner Sanctum.

Once you arrive at this territory, you see your life in a new light, a light that sheds grace on you and renders the ordinary miraculous. You may come and go from this rejuvenating oasis because, God knows, the world tugs you away from time to time; but it will always be there for you, a haven and a home that forever welcomes you.

Mallie and I had this car we loved like a baby. It was a VW Corrado V6—a small, black sports car that was sexy and could really move. When we bought it, it was a real gift to ourselves, a reward for all our good work. At first, it was Bob's car, then it became Mallie's car. But really it belonged to both of us and was somehow a sign that we had done something good and God loved us. Gradually, we paid it off and then we really owned it, not the bank. Mallie would drive it up to Vermont to visit her mom in a nursing home, and the sadness of her mom's Alzheimer's disease was at least minimally tempered by a pleasurable ride up and back.

As the little black sports car grew older, it began to develop certain ailments, as cars are wont to do. We especially noticed continuous problems with the cooling system—the radiator, thermostat, and water pump. No matter how often we repaired these problems, they seemed to recur, as though the car's immune system was particularly susceptible in these areas. When we first considered selling the car, we dismissed the thought quickly. This was our baby! Mallie continued to drive it back and forth to Vermont on a regular basis. Somehow the car and her mom, both failing slowly, had some connection. More and more, as Mallie drove the five hours back and forth, often on fairly deserted country roads, she'd keep one eye on the road and the other on the temperature gauge.

Mallie was having a hard time one day on the trip. She was driving the little black sports car and it wasn't happy. The red light was flashing, never a good sign. The temperature gauge was way up. The engine was overheating. Steam was rising from the hood. It wasn't the coolant either. Meanwhile, Mallie was trying to keep her own cool while thinking about the fact that we had only recently replaced the water pump twice, not to mention the radiator and the thermostat. Moreover, she was in the middle of nowhere, more than an hour from home, no gas station in sight. She tried to relax, her heart and her knuckles at odds. "Oh God," she thought. "You gotta help me out here. Can you hear me? I really need you. You got that? I'm having a little problem and I can't handle it by myself. Okay? I know you are very busy and have more important things on your mind than my little car here, but, please, if it wouldn't be a problem, I need you to get that red light off for me." She kept driving slowly, breathing, relaxing, drawing on her deep faith, continuing to communicate with God. "You've got to help me out here, God. Just get me home, okay? You get me home, I'll sing your praises forever. I would anyway, but please, God, give me a break. I don't ask for too much. . . . I'm waiting, God." As she crawled on, she suddenly noticed the red light go off and the temperature gauge begin to settle down. Soon the car was running fine and she managed to get home. When she told me the story, she and I both knew that God had somehow blown a gust of cool air on that little black sports car.

It was the only rational explanation.

◇ ◇ ◇ ◇

It's all very well to develop a positive image of yourself and others, but, after all is said and done, a positive image, while preferable to a negative one, is no less an image. It exists in the mind. It lives in a movie theater showing you images on the screen of your mind—written, directed, edited, and produced by none other than your mind itself. In terms of the development of your self-esteem, there comes a time when your mind is more a limitation than an asset. Who you are finally is not a product of your mind, but rather an essence, a spirit that, while unique, is connected to God. Once you have a transcendent experience of your own spiritual connection, you have a knowledge of your self that forever changes you. The question is, how can you create such an experience? Is it even possible? Or does it happen spontaneously to those of us either of remarkable good fortune or questionable sanity, depending on your point of view?

A three-year-old girl tiptoed into the nursery where her baby sister was sleeping. She looked at the peaceful face of her new sibling. "Tell me," she whispered. "Please tell me about God. I've almost forgotten."

THE SEARCH FOR INNER SANCTUM

The search for Inner Sanctum begins in the seaside town of Sleepy Cove where, choosing not to take Survival Road, you head on toward Port Wake Up, sensing there is more to life than struggle and stress. Gazing out at the Sea of Seekers, you know you are not alone on your path and you continue on to Curiosity Corner where Temptation Trail beckons you. Rejecting the lure, you head up to Stillness Valley and Revelation Lake by Peace Peak, where Sacred Ground and Essence Meadows can be viewed and your goal of Inner Sanctum is within reach.

Experiencing your divine essence, God-self, or higher self—whatever you choose to call it—is essentially a mystical experience rather than a function of religion. Many religious institutions teach that (1) God lives outside and separate from you and (2) the idea of a God existing within you is blasphemous. Such teaching is institutionally common, although the founders of many religions had personal, mystical revelations on which doctrine was later based. Most Western religions teach children that God is male, old, wise, and a kind of Super King of the universe who resides on a throne in the heavens overseeing all Creation. He rewards the good and punishes the bad, if not in this lifetime, then afterward. Many of us grew up with this image of a *super parent* who was the ultimate authority.

In my home, if my mother's disapproval didn't produce a result, if my father's punishment was ineffective, then it was the threat of God's ultimate judgment that would be brought out of the closet. "God's going to make you pay for this!" The very words would make me quiver. Certainly, God's penalty would be worse than being grounded or losing my allowance. His power was unlimited. I could burn in Hell if He thought it a just sentence. I grew up frightened of a punishing God, and it took me many years to learn the love of God. Even as an adult, when things would go bad, I would have the lingering thought that I had done some wrong and was being punished.

I think it is quite common in Western civilization to have an anthropomorphic view of God. The Greeks saw their gods as a race of superhumans who possessed human emotions and human motivations from love to jealousy, greed to generosity, vengeance to forgiveness. In the Judaic world, God is a stern, loving father with a multitude of rules and laws to guide us toward ethical behavior. In the Christian world, God is equally demanding but also perhaps more merciful and forgiving of human frailties. But in almost all Western religions, God is seen as human in form, emotion, and behavior. It's anyone's guess whether this is a projection of human beings on their creator, or simply a reflection of the belief that we are created in God's image and therefore He must resemble us.

Beyond the traditional beliefs of all religions lie the more occult, mystical traditions wherein we find more transcendental and less anthropomorphic views of God. For example, in some belief systems God is described as a presence in the universe. In others adherents believe that God is a universal energy, a binding force, an intelligent design, a unifying field, even a supreme void out of which creation in born. In the Kabbalah, God is seen as eminently present but, at the same time, deeply hidden, and ultimately unknowable. The Buddhists believe that it is from the heart of total emptiness that God manifests Himself, and that when we experience this emptiness we can access the heart of perfect wisdom and compassion. Albert Einstein, a mystic and the founder of quantum physics, believed much the same thing when he said that "everything is emptiness and all form is condensed emptiness." In the Old Testament, we learn that we were created out of dust, while in the New Testament Jesus tells us that we shall do even greater things than He (a strange statement if we are doomed to a life of sin and repentance).

Many Native American religions assert that God lives in the earth. The Hopis' kivas are temples where the holiest point is the lowest on earth, as opposed to magnificent cathedrals in other traditions whose spires point toward the heavens.

As you can see, our ancestors have come up with a tremendous variety of descriptions of God, many of which include the possibility for inner access to God rather than interminable separation from Him.

◇ ◇ ◇ ◇

I was interviewing my grandsons Sam and Jake about God. I asked them if they thought God was invisible. "No," said Jake. "God is everything so he can't be invisible." Sam, the older one, saw it differently: "I think God is both visible and invisible." I proceeded to ask if they thought God created everything. They both said yes. When I pressed them and asked if God created bad things as well as good, they stopped and thought for a moment. "No," said Jake, "only the good things." "I think he created both," Sam suggested. "But why?" I asked. Sam, nine at the time, scratched his chin, then replied, "He wanted to give us challenges."

◇ ◇ ◇ ◇

The way to God is deeply personal and as unpredictable as life itself. While the religions of the world at their best serve as communities that bind people together in ritual, prayer, and hope, the direct experience of God can occur in nature as well as churches, in living rooms as well as mosques, in hospitals as well as temples. Each person's path is personal, highly unique, a result of her own choices and consequences, with unusual twists and turns, land mines, and lessons along the way. The Light of God can shine on anyone at any time. Revelation can come in one Holy Instant, or in bits and pieces. While there are practices one can do to increase the probability of having a direct experience of God, there are no guarantees.

You can meditate and look within.

You can visit sacred sites and look without.

You can commune with nature.

You can chant mantras.

You can do yoga.

You can practice martial arts.

You can gaze on holy images.

You can participate in rituals.

You can breathe and you can have rebirthing sessions.

You can go to your church, temple, or mosque.

And you can do all these things and still not see the Light. Or, you could be hanging the laundry out to dry, and, lo and behold, enlightenment strikes!

PORT WAKE UP

You wake up one morning and sense it is different from all other mornings. You take a deep breath and feel something coming back to you, some long-lost part. Spontaneously, you thank God for the return of your wandering soul, and then you breathe slowly and fully for several minutes. You get dressed and head down to Port Wake Up by the Sea of Seekers. The place is hopping and there is electricity in the air. You ask what's happening, and the waitress points out to sea where you notice a big old schooner entering the harbor.

You look more carefully and observe hordes of people on the deck of the boat. You ask who they are, and the waitress says, "Seekers. Like all of us. Looking for the Source. Every day a new boat arrives, full of people who just wake up that morning and want something more out of life, something sacred." You nod your head, knowing exactly what she means.

It is not hard work, struggle, sacrifice, and discipline that necessarily lead to the Light. Nor is it laziness, idleness, disorganization, and chaos that pave the path to God. Finding God is not separate from finding joy, because it is the joy of life that is the experience of God. If you don't love your life, how will you find the Creator? If you think life is a punishment and not a gift, how will you find grace? And if you feel that life owes you something, where will this God who is in debt to you reside? In your heart? In your head? In your portfolio? Dream on.

Part of the problem lies in our mistaken notion of the miraculous. We grow up with a mythology about miracles, thinking they must mean walking on water, the parting of a sea, or immaculate conception. Yet we live in an age of modern marvels. We are numbed by the onslaught of miraculous events. We have built bridges, tunnels, and skyscrapers that were once unimaginable. We have landed men on the moon, transplanted organs, cloned sheep, and saved the lives of countless premature babies as well as terminally ill adults. What would have been considered extraordinary a century years ago—supersonic airplanes, high-speed levitating trains, the Internet, and robotics—is now commonplace.

We live in an age of such "ordinary miracles"—indeed, every age has its own such miracles—that we often just witness them as blurs going by as we focus our attention on more important things, whether they be the stock market, sports, Hollywood, or the World Wide Web. It has been said and seems to be true that there is no "degree" of miracles. If you're looking for the big ones, you're likely to miss the everyday ones. If you think that miracles are a myth or merely a collective memory of a more miraculous age, you are unlikely to be open to experiencing them now. Moreover, if you are stuck in a belief that you will never experience the miraculous, you are blocking your own connection to the divine. And if you don't even entertain the possibility that you yourself could be on sacred ground, you leave yourself alone and confused, thinking, in John Donne's words, you are an island and not a part of a continent. Once you open the door to your inner sanctum, you will experience a larger you, a you connected to all and everything. You will find yourself and experience what *is* at that moment: a flash of the universe in a chosen personal moment. Cosmic intimacy.

◇ ◇ ◇ ◇

I was facilitating a group, and people were sharing decisions they made about God as a child.

"God is a man," said one woman. "I'll always be separate from Him."

"God lives in nature, not in the city."

"God is unfair. Good people suffer and bad people are rewarded."

"God is merciful."

"God is a good listener."

"God doesn't have enough time to answer everyone's prayers."

"God is love."

"God is like an absentee landlord. He is nowhere to be found when you have a complaint."

"God is everywhere."

◇ ◇ ◇ ◇

We tend to look for God in all the wrong places. Or at least we skip the most important place of all. Many can see Him in a starlit night, a rainbow, a sunset, or a spider spinning its web. Others can see Him in the highest mountain, the deepest ocean, the rain forests and the savannas, the deserts and the polar ice caps. Or in an endangered species—a soaring eagle, a singing dolphin, a fluttering butterfly. Some can even see God in man, or in some men more than others, or in men but not women perhaps—in priests, martyrs, saints, and gurus. Or in the face of a newborn child. But usually, and sadly, the last person whose face you recognize as a piece of God is you yourself.

Even your physical body is God in action. Think of it: billions of molecules in constant intelligent activity, 97 percent of them completely new every thirteen months. Billions of cells, governed by little "brains" within, communicating, cooperating, and co-creating wellness for the whole entity. When one part suffers injury, the entire body begins an amazing summoning of energy, resources, and intelligence to create healing for that local wound. Would that the whole world, or even a single family, could demonstrate such wisdom, compassion, effectiveness, and mastery of relationships. How can a human being even come to be without a miracle? How can two cells transform into a full-fledged person in such a short time? Some say it's genetics. I say that behind the DNA lies an unseen design and stands the most brilliant of all designers, the Supreme Architect of genetic engineering and, indeed, of the whole universe. I call Him or Her or It *God*. Perhaps He prefers to be known as the Nameless One. Either way, I feel His presence all around me and within me. Without Him, without that Infinite Intelligence, I know that everything would cave into the endless emptiness again.

Several years ago I read about a scandal in Newark, New Jersey. It was Christmas time and a local theater was rehearsing a theatrical pageant to celebrate the passion of Christ. The man playing the role of Jesus suddenly found himself the center of controversy. He began receiving hate mail, threats on his life, vitriol from ignorant people irate that he had the audacity to play the part of the Son of God. And what was the problem? Why was this innocent man subjected to such hatred and scorn? It just so happened this actor was African American. And everyone knew that Jesus was Caucasian!

◇ ◇ ◇ ◇

Mallie seeks out the Black Madonna. She believes that the black virgin is a fertility symbol. Several times, when friends of ours have had trouble conceiving, she has found them Black Madonnas to meditate on. Usually, a child is conceived or adopted soon after. When we realize that the complexion of Jesus, a Jew born in Bethlehem, was probably fairly swarthy, and how his image was redone by the PR branch of the Christian church, not to mention Renaissance painters, it is easy to come to the conclusion that not only God but also Jesus has been "created" in the image of a Caucasian man, partly for the purpose of crusading Christian beliefs, politics, and power throughout the so-called pagan world.

If we believe that God exists more in some of us than in others, what are we saying? That God is omnipresent, but not equally so? That God withholds Himself from one part of Creation and dispenses more of Himself to other parts? How can we divide our notion of God, chopping Him up and dishing Him out according to our prejudices, and then call that religion, spirituality, or even common sense? If there is a God, He is everywhere. He may be hiding, but He is nevertheless present, self-evident in so many ways. And, in the final analysis, we may be hiding from Him a whole lot more than He is hiding from us.

Find your Inner Sanctum. Honor your sacred ground. Most of us now feel that we live in a sacred environment and that if we don't honor it, it will not honor us. Of course, many primitive societies have known this forever. Cultures that identify spirit more with the earth than with heaven tend to notice the rhythms and cycles of their environment more, usually replenishing the earth when they take from it. The Kahuna priests of Hawai'i urge us never to move the slightest piece of earth, a pebble, a speck of dust, from one place to another without asking permission from the Creator. Transgression can be very subtle, but very significant in its consequences. Of course, if you believe that God lives far away in the sky, it is easier to litter, dump garbage, pollute the air and water with toxic waste. Is this planet a dumping ground, a vast garbage heap? Or is it sacred to us and do we need to listen to its needs as well as our own, which are not separate in the long run. Is the earth alive or dead? And if it is alive, how can any God be apart from it?

Sacred ground exists both in our hearts and under our feet.

◇ ◇ ◇ ◇

Jake was discussing God with a preschool friend. They were sitting at the kitchen table. Tracy was expressing her point of view that God lived in heaven and if she was good when she died she would be with Him. Jake thought about this idea, as he thinks deeply about many things. "No," he finally said. "God is everywhere, in everything. God is even in this table."

I was with a group inside the Great Pyramid of Giza. It was early in the morning and we had gained private use of the inner sanctum for a meditation. We sat on the stone floor and smelled thousands of years of mystery. It was so dark that when I closed my eyes it didn't get any darker. A man in the group blew a didgeridoo, which hauntingly echoed throughout the corridors and spaces. After some time I slowly opened my eyes, anticipating pitch blackness, but instead saw a glowing light within each person. At first I couldn't believe my eyes because I knew what I was seeing had no rational explanation. I closed my eyes and opened them again. No doubt about it: everyone was illuminated.

◇ ◇ ◇ ◇

It is no accident that the origin of religion on this planet lies in fertility rites that celebrated the seasons. Spring planting. Fall harvest. The journey from seed to feed. The very act of Creation was honored as Mother Earth herself gave birth to what nourished Her offspring. This is why so many early spiritual festivities were sexual in tone. Creativity and sexuality are ultimately one and the same. And just as a child naturally looks up to a parent, Spirit always seeks to honor its Creator. The possibility of a Creator's existing as separate from His Creation makes no more sense than a parent feeling that his existence does not continue in his child. Almost any artist, sculptor, musician, or writer will tell you that a piece of himself or herself lives in the Created. So it is with human beings: a part of God lives in us all—not all of God in each of us, but a part in all.

SACRED GROUND

Create a sacred place in your home, a place dedicated to the renewal of your spirit and the search for Inner Sanctum. Create a space that represents you at your best, as well as your connection to the infinite. Have a good picture of yourself, and objects that give you energy. Include photographs of inspirational people and loved ones, as well as books that lead you to higher ground. Keep in mind, it does not have to be a "religious" space, but it should represent the joy of being you. It should be a place that you love to go to and, when you sit there for twenty minutes every day, you tend to feel a smile breaking out on your face.

Honor your sacred essence. It is the core of your being, the heart of your Self. It is where God lives in you. Even if you cannot experience it, have a sense of it lying hidden just beyond your grasp. Become aware of the great mystery. It is this sacred ground that you seek most of all, not all the other material things you think will fill up the emptiness within you. In a sense, all our addictions are substitutes for this feeling of God within us. We mistakenly think we can find the fullness of life by satisfying our desires and obsessions, but all these attractions—money, sex, drugs, alcohol, sugar, TV, computers—all of them are ultimately like junk food, giving gratification immediately but a lingering sensation of dissatisfaction. The mother of all addictions is this addiction to thinking you are separate from both God and the resulting endless emptiness you dread feeling. The alternative is to go into that void and meet the God you have been hiding from on His own sacred ground.

He awaits you, if not at the gate, then at any turn of your path, be it a mountain, a bush, a river, or a manger. Keep your eyes open. Or closed.

He lives in your breath as well. In almost every language, the word for *breath* and the word for *spirit* are connected at the root. Respiration and spirit. Why is that? Even in the book of Genesis we are told that God breathed life into man. Before the breath, man was just a lump of clay. In the Kabbalah we are urged every morning to take a breath and thank God for returning our wandering souls to our bodies. So it is, in many of my sessions, clients are having spiritual experiences while they are doing breathwork therapy. Many of them claim to see the Light. Is it the light at the end of the birth canal? Is it the Light of God? Are they hypnotized by oxygenation into some kind of transcendental trance? I cannot say for sure. But I cannot easily dismiss or deny the validity of a completely rational human being who, after breathing intensely for one hour, says to me in total lucidity, "I felt God was with me."

One of the most fundamental of all human rights is the freedom to worship as one chooses. While such a right is an essential basis for tolerance and coexistence, a more fundamental right lies in honoring the worshipper's own sacred self. As long as mankind insists on believing that God is separate from the human family, that same belief in separation will tend to erupt in crusades, jihads, persecution, and holy wars. It is only when we entertain a new paradigm—which holds the quantum belief that we all exist in God and God exists in all of us—that we will lay the foundation for a world of real love, compassion, and tolerance. God contains you and you incarnate God.

◇ ◇ ◇ ◇

Go on a vision quest once in a while. Often, in my programs, I ask each participant to do a vision quest, that is, conduct a solo experience in nature for three days. Go sit on a rock or a mountain top, or by a river or a shore, and listen, look. Wait. Maybe you will see something you've never seen before. Maybe a voice will come to you. Or a guide will reveal a secret. Or your mission for this lifetime will become clear to you. On the other hand, maybe it will start pouring and you will run to your tent.

I remember visiting Jerusalem for the first time. No sooner had I set foot on the stone streets of the ancient city, layer upon layer of civilization beneath the surface, than my heart began pounding like a ceremonial drum beckoning me.

Of course, God might be staring you right in the face. In your own backyard. Your sacred ground calls to you from your immediate world as well as faraway lands. Your connection to a personal spot can heighten your sense of your sacred self. For example, perhaps you have a garden that nurtures your roots, a tree that calls to you, a special boulder you like to sit on, a stream to sit by. Or maybe it's a window you like looking out, an altar to gaze at, a particular chair that comforts your soul. Allow such sacred spaces to exert their pull on you. They draw you to something deep in yourself that needs attention.

I remember as a teenager, I would avoid the rabbi when he came walking down the street. He was a huge, towering man, who frightened me to death. He had called me into his office shortly before my bar mitzvah, explaining to me the significance of this event in my life and asking me to promise to be a good Jew, perhaps even a cantor or a rabbi myself. I promised. Afterward, I drifted away from the synagogue and into secular activities. When I would see him lumbering down the sidewalk, I would sneak across the street to avoid his scrutiny. I wanted to hide from this holy man, to whom I had promised my soul but from whom I had then drifted away. Finally, one day, when I was seventeen and preparing to go off to college, I saw him coming toward me again. I crossed the street. So did he. He waved at me and I could no longer avoid him. In truth, he didn't seem quite so big anymore, although I still had to look up to him. Then he smiled, congratulating me on going to a good college. How did he know? He ran a hand through my hair and told me I was a good boy no matter what. He said it didn't matter if I was a rabbi or a scientist, a cantor or a doctor. God loved me no matter what. I was so moved I had to fight back the tears. I gave him an awkward hug, and he told me to tell my parents I was a good boy. He laughed as I went off.

◆ ◆ ◆ ◆

One day I had to call the old synagogue. I needed a document about my mother's burial plot. I could hear my heart pumping as the telephone was ringing. A woman answered and, when I told her what I wanted, she put me through to the rabbi. He asked me who I was and when I told him, he laughed. He asked me everything about my life, my mother and father. I was amazed by his open heart and phenomenal memory. As I was getting off the phone, he said to me, "Don't forget. You are blessed by God."

Aren't we all?

The Pitfall

The *pitfall* here is that you get lost on "the God trip." You become so full of your God-self that you think you *are* God Almighty rather than just another natural piece of God's sacred territory. You can develop a special relationship with God, thinking He loves you exclusively. You can come down with a serious case of spiritual egotism, thinking you are superior to others because of your spiritual ascendance and therefore relegating others to an inferior rung on the ladder of spiritual evolution. Such a superiority complex is often a signal that you are overcompensating for deep feelings of inferiority. Perhaps you have become a "spiritual climber," as some people become social climbers, and you are seeking recognition outside yourself in obscure spiritual practices. For example, someone who feels totally rejected in life can invent an "alien psychology" alter ego. He might claim that he has been chosen for a very important mission by leaders of an advanced race from a distant galaxy. Intergalactic overcompensation! Or, he can apply the same attitude to invented past lives, regressing to false memories of fame and fortune from ancient eras. Also, one might be running the same old pattern of projecting his low self-esteem on others, denying his feelings and pretending that he is God and everyone else is not.

If you find yourself locked into this perception, it is a sign that you need to backtrack to Journeys 2 and 6, and pay close attention to each step along the path. Remember, as long as you are viewing others as less than you, whether less intelligent, less good, or less spiritual, you are living in your judgments and not really seeing the actual person. And as long as you need to put people down to lift yourself up in your own estimation, you are mistaking high self-esteem for being full of yourself. So get off your high horse and realize that just because God lives in you doesn't make you a penthouse and everyone else a basement or garage. God happily resides in each of us, poor or rich. He sleeps in every house, flat, tent, or teepee that exists on earth. None of us are more special than our family members, neighbors, friends, and even complete strangers.

Steps on the Seventh Journey

1. Be curious. See yourself as a seeker.
2. Feel your attraction to what connects you to the universe.
3. Be open to sudden revelations.
4. Surround yourself with objects that give you energy.
5. Look at the beauty of nature.
6. Notice the magical moments in your life.
7. Listen to beautiful music.
8. Read inspirational books.
9. Develop a sense of the miraculous—see the ordinary as extraordinary.
10. Distinguish between personal spirituality and religion.
11. Be still. Listen in silence.

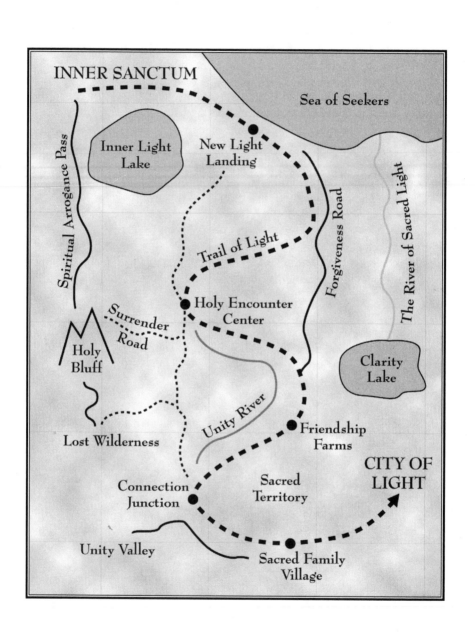

INNER SANCTUM

Sea of Seekers

Spiritual Arrogance Pass

Inner Light Lake

New Light Landing

The River of Sacred Light

Trail of Light

Forgiveness Road

Surrender Road

Holy Encounter Center

Holy Bluff

Clarity Lake

Unity River

Lost Wilderness

Friendship Farms

CITY OF LIGHT

Connection Junction

Sacred Territory

Unity Valley

Sacred Family Village

Journey 8

The Trail of Light in Others

Since all of life is sacred, including you yourself, the people you meet on your journey home are also sacred. Your return to self is a trail of light supplied by the divine inner radiance of those you encounter on the path. It is important to recognize the sacred in others both for your own progress and for theirs. To feel as if you carry an exclusive light within you separates you from humankind, which excludes you from connections vital to your self-realization. To allow a few other individuals into your special circle, recognizing their divinity along with your own, is an improvement but still leaves you incomplete. It is when you honor the sacred in all that the circle of light is fully reflected within yourself. It is when you see all of humanity as your sacred family that you claim the totality of your own inner sanctum.

Many people seem anything *but* sacred. God knows, there seem to be some pretty bad people out there, doing anything but sacred deeds. It can be extremely tempting to divide the world into a war between good and evil, and count yourself among God's chosen ones. The problem with this view of the world is that once you make such a division, you become very much like many of those you judge, anointing yourself as virtuous and seeing evil outside yourself.

God has no favorites, and spirit is democratically distributed among all His children. When people act in abominable ways, we of course condemn their behavior, and in the court of humankind we might punish them appropriately. In the higher court, however, we recognize that while some souls are more warped, twisted, and tormented than others, every soul contains light and every soul is crying for some form of acknowledgment, recognition, and love.

As you greet people on your journey, look for the light they contain. You might have to deal with a few shadows from time to time, as others might have to deal with yours. Nonetheless, if you think of yourself as a gatherer of light, when you return home you will be at home not only with your whole self but also with your entire sacred family.

◇ ◇ ◇ ◇ ◇ ◇ ◇ ◇ ◇ ◇

Janet and Rebecca were mother and daughter, and they weren't getting along very well. Janet was in her forties and Rebecca in her twenties, and the generation gap between them resembled the Grand Canyon. Janet, a single mother (Rebecca's father died when she was three), just couldn't understand her daughter's lack of motivation in life. She herself had worked hard since she graduated from college, never having the luxury of laziness. Therefore, she saw Rebecca's dropping out of school, living at home, hanging out with a suspect group of friends, and not even picking up after herself as extremely inappropriate behavior. Rebecca, for her part, felt completely misunderstood by her mom, unsupported, unloved, and unwanted, which in fact she had been at her birth.

Rebecca didn't want to come to my seminar. Her mother had insisted, especially after Rebecca had driven the car into a tree the week before. At the first break, they both came up to me. They were like two cats going at it. Rebecca said she wanted to go home. Janet replied that if she went home, she could start packing. Rebecca thought that sounded like a good idea. Janet reminded her she had no place else to go, whereupon Rebecca said that living on the street was better than living with a mother who didn't love her. That did it. Janet broke down in tears. I explained that the seminar was voluntary and if Rebecca was not there of her own volition, there was no point in her staying. Janet understood this but still wanted me to fix her daughter. I suggested that Rebecca go out of the hotel, take a long walk, and only come back if she really wanted to be there for herself. I urged her to really be honest with herself and not just quit because she wanted to spite her mom. She nodded and left.

A couple of hours passed and Rebecca returned to the seminar. She had a completely different point of view now that she was choosing to be there rather than forced into coming. When I talked about birth, she shared that she was an induced birth and that her father had wanted a boy. Later, she volunteered that she tended to attract men who were like her father, not there for her in any meaningful way. Her father had died, and other men either were dead emotionally or else they abandoned her. Meanwhile, Janet, her mother, said little, sitting quietly in the back row.

When I began to discuss forgiveness, both Rebecca and Janet welled up with tears. After the process, Rebecca shared that she had been blaming her mother because she was too afraid to confront her feelings about her father, the one she was really angry at. Janet owned that she was guilt-ridden and felt like a failure as a single mother. Moreover, she felt that Rebecca loved her dead father more than her live mother. When they embraced each other, the whole room broke down in tears. Even I was waving my hand for a Kleenex.

Rebecca was crying. She was in a group breathing session and was remembering her father's death when she was three. "He left me," she cried. "Why? What did I do wrong?" I gently placed a hand on her head. "Nothing," I said. "He died because he died, not because of anything you did or didn't do." She breathed some more. Then she exploded, "I am so furious at him for dying! He had no right!" I knew it was important she breathe out her resentment, or else she would never forgive him. Later, after the session, she was sharing with her mother. They were so connected, facing each other. I could see mother and daughter bonded in light. Afterward, Rebecca said to the whole group, "I never realized what a great mom I had until today. I thought my dad was great and he died. So my mom couldn't be great because she was alive. And I wanted to be dead like my dad. Now I can see the light in my mother. Look at her. She is so beautiful! She has the light of God shining in her eyes. And she's alive. I am so fantastically lucky to have a mother like this!" Kleenex time again.

◇ ◇ ◇ ◇

Honoring the sacred ground within you paves the way to seeing God's presence in others as well. When you extend this experience of your own divinity to your mate, children, parents, siblings, friends, and, indeed, to complete strangers, you find that your self-awareness stretches in the process. Suddenly, you feel the interconnectedness of all of humanity, even all of life. You take your place in the great circle of divine beingness that contains us all.

THE TRAIL OF LIGHT IN OTHERS

The trail of light in others begins at Inner Sanctum and turns at New Light Landing, where you begin to see others in a new light. You continue down the road to Holy Encounter Center, where you recognize every meeting with another human being as an opportunity to exchange love and light. At Friendship Farms you grow new relationships, spiritual hybrids combining the best qualities in you with the best in others. You're in Sacred Territory now, and at Connection Junction you can literally see the light in other people, connecting from essence to essence instead of from personality to personality. When you arrive at Sacred Family Village, you not only recognize the light in all your family members but also you see all humanity as global villagers, your extended family of light. On entering the City of Light, you are amazed by the brilliance of so many lightbeings sharing one space, and amazed by how much light you have gathered on the trail.

It can be difficult to see the God in someone who is unaware of his own sacred ground, but it is important nonetheless. Sometimes, when you are reacting negatively to another person, it is simply a matter of your reflexes being triggered by another person's ignorant beliefs or behaviors. When you are tempted to react in such a manner, it is always a good idea to take a breath or two first. In just one breath you can open a window of opportunity to alternative responses. Ultimately, responsibility is the ability to respond differently. You have this ability, but it is useless unless you use it.

Sometimes I ask myself how God would react to such a situation. Or, even better, if I were talking to God, what would I say? Of course, my mind says, "Well, God would never do something so stupid." Yet we are all God. We all have the ability to take our divine essence and act incredibly stupidly. When you condemn another person, what are you really saying? That you are superior to him? That his essence is less than yours? The trick is to relate to the essence of a person even when you find his behavior atrocious.

This is especially true with children. I have already mentioned the importance of speaking to the intelligence of a child. Avoid the temptation to condemn your child when he makes mistakes. We all make mistakes. We all have been children. If your child is behaving perfectly because he is terrified of displeasing you, you might have a bigger problem than with the normal child who slips up once in a while. Teach your child self-correcting techniques rather than confronting him with a feeling of inadequacy. Most of all, remember whom you're talking to. This child is not merely a lump of clay. He is, as you are, a spark of divine light, a messenger from God, an angel of love.

In any relationship, it is the same. When two people have recognized their own sacred ground and, at the same time, honor that space in each other, problems become easier to resolve and conflicts seem less significant. Two people who recognize their own and each other's divinity are literally living in a temple of love. There is a dignity about such a relationship. A state of grace is born from this sacred recognition.

NEW LIGHT LANDING

Sit somewhere where you are comfortable. Relax your body. Visualize in the space in front of you someone with whom you have a difficult relationship. See the person as clearly as possible, but, as with any visualization, don't force the image; allow it to emerge. When you have a good picture in your mind, say to yourself, "I am willing to see _____ in a new light." Then imagine a golden pyramid hovering above the head of this person, golden light streaming down into his or her crown, and down throughout his or her entire body. Imagine this person as a vehicle for pure golden light. Take a few good breaths and say silently to this person, "God bless you, my friend."

People deserve to be respected for who they are. Just as you want to be treated properly, the next person also is worthy of that same respect from you. Respect exists on many levels. You can respect a person for what she does, what she believes, or what she feels. You can respect her simply because she is a person and all people merit respect. The level of respect I'm referring to goes beyond these other levels. I am saying we should respect others because they are sacred beings. They might not look sacred or act sacred all the time. They might not have the same sacred language that you do. Nevertheless, at the core every human being is a celebration of that same sacred energy. We are all bound together by it. There is nothing separate from it.

Finally, the reason to look for the God in others is not just that they deserve that level of respect from you. No, it is that you grow in the process. When you see others in the darkness of their shadows, you choose to live in that darkness with them. When, on the other hand, you see past the shadow and notice the light that casts the shadow, then you live in the light of that being. And seeing the light in another, your light expands. In a spiritual sense, you need that other person's sacred ground to continue your journey home to yourself. The light of the world shines for you. It shows you the way, and it gives you hope. Alone, you are a mere flicker of possibility. Joined to the light of the world, your radiance is unlimited.

My grandson Jake has a lot of God in him. Along with a fair amount of devil. When he feels a little inadequate because of his physical limitations (he has a ten-year-old brother) and he needs to assert his power, he will frequently say things like, "When I was an adult, I was able to do that," or "When I was a grown-up, I knew the answer to that." The other day he said, "When I was in the land I was at before I came here. . . ." He has a sense of the eternality of his life, not to mention some interesting past lives. When I look at him, I see an ancient soul in a little body. I see a huge presence that extends far beyond his physical boundaries. Call it an aura, a halo, or an energy body framing the physical one. Whatever it is, we all have it. Look for it when you look at your children, your parents, your mate. Friends and strangers as well. Everyone has a glow, a radiance. As with beauty, this light is seen from the eye of the beholder. When you shed this light on another, you see him as he is, not a limited physical container but, rather, a flowing river of electrical energy.

◇ ◇ ◇ ◇

If God is in everyone, why is there such evil in the world? Why didn't God just create a perfect world without any violence, hunger, poverty, disease, and death? What's going on here? Look at the world. It certainly doesn't seem like a work of God. When you see six-year-old children taking guns to school and killing other children, it is difficult to see God as alive and well on this earth. What's the explanation? Is it the devil at work? Is it human nature? Is it the failure of the family unit? Is it Darwin's survival of the fittest? Is it the money motive? Is it a sign of the psychological stress of the times? Maybe it's all the environmental damage catching up to our brains. Who can say for sure?

There is a story in the Kabbalah that goes like this. In the beginning God created a totally perfect world. There was only one problem: because it was perfect, it could not change. If it changed, it would no longer be perfect. So it had to remain static, always the same, no room for improvement. Eventually, this static world atrophied and died. It caved in on itself. God thought about this for some time, then came up with a better idea. He created an imperfect world, where human beings had free will, the capacity to make mistakes and learn from them. God created this second world as a massive self-improvement project. And the greatest gift he gave humans to transform his world was forgiveness. It is through forgiveness that we ultimately become self-realized and, in a sense, can save this world. This was the teaching of Abraham, Jesus, Muhammad, Buddha, and all the great spiritual leaders who have graced this earth. Forgiveness sets us free.

It is through forgiveness that you are transformed. And when you forgive another, you see him in the light of your love again. Having returned to love, you recognize that God too has returned to His sacred ground within the other person. Divinity is restored to its internal throne. While all this may sound spiritually correct and might even be true, how do you actually forgive another person? What does forgiveness really mean?

Many people think they can just say the words, "I forgive you," and magically wipe away all resentment, blame, and anger. Would that it were so simple. Then there is the theory that there is really nothing to forgive, since we are all innocent and responsible for our own actions, experiences, pleasures, and pain in this life. That sounds a little too easy as well. The fact is that when you feel wronged by another, you have many feelings that need to be felt, sorted out, and resolved before you can actually proceed to those magic words, "I forgive you."

◇ ◇ ◇ ◇

Tristan was trying to forgive his mother. The trouble was, he couldn't even feel his anger. He knew something was wrong because he always felt a coldness with her, but his adult mind told him she had done the best she could. Moreover, whenever he questioned her about his early development, she replied that everything was perfectly normal and nothing unusual had happened.

Tristan was also trying to understand why he was entangled in a very difficult relationship with a woman whom he had known for a year and who, since moving in with him, had revealed some serious emotional and mental problems. Confessing that he always had a tendency toward co-dependent relationships, he admitted that it had never been so strong as with his current partner. He sensed that his relationship with her was being affected by unresolved material with his mother.

Tristan was working with me for ten days during an advanced intensive training program. He lived on the West Coast but had grown up near New York City. He met his parents one day for dinner early in the program. The next morning he said that they had once again stated that his birth and childhood had been very normal. Nothing special.

During the week Tristan went through several powerful "rebirth" experiences in water. He accessed the memory that his mother had had a miscarriage shortly before he was conceived. When I mentioned the "ghost womb" theory (if the mother does not complete the mourning for a miscarried child, that grief can stay in the womb), he nodded. In one session, he became aware that when he was in the womb his mother was depressed and worried about his survival. He felt he began taking care of her even then, repressing his own needs and sending her messages that he was okay.

In another meeting, Tristan was doing a process with a very loving, smothering, and chaotic woman. Her caring and inadequacy brought up Tristan's rage toward his mother. He shared that he never had his own space as a child, and at a certain point put up a hammock in the backyard that became his space.

Tristan did brilliant work on himself all week. He wrote a "completion letter" to his mother, cut his energy cord with her, and revisited scenes from his childhood, using *innerventions* to gain closure. Toward the end of the intensive he once again met his parents for dinner. The next morning he shared with us that his mother confirmed everything he had experienced, including the miscarriage, her feelings while he was in the womb, and events early in his life. Tristan concluded by telling us that his mother seemed a transformed person, warm, with softness in her eyes. She was radiant.

The truth was, Tristan's forgiveness had set him free, enabling him to see the light of God in his mother.

Be careful not to deceive yourself into false forgiveness. If you forgive with your mind only, not with your heart and soul, you are more likely to attract similar situations again. So, by all means, feel everything you need to feel. Try to understand where all your feelings are coming from. Go through them all and, when you're done, let them go. And remember, you deserve better. Don't wallow in the pain or the shame. Move out into the light at the first available opportunity.

Some things seem unforgivable, and perhaps are. Think of the Holocaust, the Inquisition, slavery or genocide of any kind. Should we simply forget all these atrocities and assume they will never recur? How can we? But perhaps even more difficult to forgive is a personal nightmare, an act of violence, abuse, or betrayal at the hands of someone you trusted. Nevertheless, if you are in love with someone and have lost sight of the sacred ground she occupies, forgiveness is probably the road back to the sanctity of your relationship.

Of course, if you have been unfairly treated as a child, you will have a greater tendency to project a sense of injustice on the world. You will feel the pain of your own abuse whenever you see a hungry child, a homeless refugee, a raped woman, or a wounded soldier. Your own wounds will open, bleeding in sympathy to images that come down on you. You will be blinded to the sacred ground in others by your own scars and fears. Your own feelings of being a victim will resonate to all the suffering you see in the world. How can you forgive Hitler when you can't even forgive your own father for his more intimate atrocities?

I remind you, there's a piece of Hitler and a piece of Christ in all of us.

❖ ❖ ❖ ❖

The other side of forgiving is saying you're sorry. There is an old myth that "Love is never having to say you're sorry." In New Age groups, in particular, there is often the doctrine that there are no accidents, all there is is love and lessons, and everyone is 100 percent responsible for their life so what's to say you're sorry for? As with forgiveness, common sense and spiritual correctness are at odds here. If you have said something, or behaved in a certain way, that severs the bond of trust between you and a loved one, saying you're sorry is not only the proper thing to do; it is the practical course of action.

I know there's no such thing as perfect parents. We all blow it once in a while. You've had a rough day and suddenly, out of the blue, you're taking it out on your five-year-old kid for a fairly minor infraction on his part. You're venting. You're taking out your frustrations on an innocent bystander, someone who, moreover, loves you forever, is a safe target, and will probably think he really did do something terrible to bring about such fury. Okay. We all do it. It's normal. It happens. Don't die over it. But get a grip. As soon as you realize what you've done, don't dig a bigger hole for yourself. Apologize to the child. Saying you're sorry won't completely undo the harm you have done, but it will change the energy and go a long way toward making reparation. Make sure that child understands he was an innocent bystander, who just happened to be in the wrong place at the wrong time. And please, don't say, "Mommy's having a hard day and she didn't mean to scream at you." Use the first person—if a parent takes responsibility rather than speaking in generalities, she communicates the message of personal accountability to her child. Say, "I was very wrong to scream at you like that and I am terribly sorry. I want you to know you didn't do anything wrong. I hope you will forgive me."

It's the same thing with a parent or a mate. If you are rude, don't defend your rudeness. Apologize. If you behave in a completely inappropriate way toward anyone, by all means tell her you are sorry. Don't go into denial of your guilt and pretend that it's the other person's fault that you hurt her. If you really love someone and you contribute to her pain, you feel what she feels because your heart is open in the relationship. You see God suffering. That's not guilt; it's compassion. Guilt is when you're so busy thinking it's your fault, you make the situation all about you—your innocence, defense, and acquittal is all you care about. But when you extend yourself to someone else, in the true meaning of love, how can you not have empathy for what she feels? And if your words or actions have resulted in such pain, how could you avoid saying you're sorry and still be honest with yourself?

Being a forgiving person, as well as one who can say you're sorry, unlocks the window to your own sacred ground and the divinity of others.

◇ ◇ ◇ ◇

Dr. Williamson was an obstetrician who had delivered thousands of babies over the course of several decades. He had been well educated at one of the prominent medical schools in his country, Holland, and was considered to be at the top of his profession. He delivered each baby as he had been taught, considering the mother's health and comfort, usually anesthetizing her to spare her pain, often performing planned inductions or C-sections because such deliveries seemed easier than nature's way, and certainly made for easier scheduling. He never gave one thought to the child, except to do his best to make sure the baby survived. In his mind, a baby didn't have a whole lot of complex feelings, and, besides, he was not yet an intelligent being. He would never remember the struggle of his birth once he grew up.

One day Dr. Williamson was delivering a baby with forceps when the newborn let out a huge howl. The doctor was stopped in his tracks. He held the baby up to look at him. The little person looked right back at him. "Oh, my God," Dr. Williamson said, "what have I done?"

The doctor suddenly realized that the child was intelligent, that there was a living soul in that little body, and that all the other babies he had delivered had living souls in them. He looked at the baby and smiled. "Thank you, child," he said.

From that day on, the doctor delivered babies differently, gently, talking to them in the womb, playing Mozart for them during delivery, and respecting the spirit of both mother and child.

◇ ◇ ◇ ◇

I've mentioned my aging mother before. Did I tell you how beautiful she was? I have photographs of her from the '20s, when she was in her prime. She was a knockout: great body, beautiful face, legs eager to hit the dance floor. Nowadays, she can hardly move. She tells the nurses, "Ninety-five sucks." Her body is a huge burden and it takes all her energy to get dressed in the morning. Whenever I'm with her, she asks me to tie her shoelaces.

112

She's still beautiful to me. When I look into her eyes, I see the light of her soul. When she laughs, I hear the lightness of her heart. And when she smiles, she still lights up the world. I've come to see that this living light is the light of God, and it exists in all of us from before we were born till after we die.

The sacred is in the "I" of the beholder, reflected in the "I" of the beheld.

Seeing the God in others is not seeing what is invisible. If you really look at what's there, the physical becomes spiritual in a flash. If you look beyond your normal way of looking, if you take the time to relax your eyes and see clearly, you can be amazed by the sacred energy you behold. It's there, a mere spark perhaps, or a brilliant emanation, but it's there. Sure as God.

CONNECTION JUNCTION

Sit opposite a friend who is willing to do this exercise with you. Make sure you are sitting in a comfortable space, and play inspirational music in the background. Light a candle and place it between you. In silence breathe together for a few moments. Place your awareness on your divine inner essence and then imagine your essence expanding and connecting with the essence of your friend. Look at the light in your friend's eyes. Feel how your own sacred ground and your friend's sacred ground combine to enlarge your sense of the divine. Let your light shine.

Sometimes, we see God in holy men or women. What is a guru? Why are so many people drawn to gurus these days? It seems clear that people have a strong need to worship the sacred in some form. What with so much corruption, pollution, and annihilation surrounding us, we seek spiritual answers in those who claim to be experts, masters, voices of God. A guru can be a person who reminds you of the God within. He can be a bridge for you to find that same God within yourself. If you have a proper relationship with such a person, it can empower you in valuable ways. As with everything, if you are out of balance in your spiritual adoration, you can experience a further loss of self rather than return to self.

In each of us, there is a "true believer" and a "skeptic." Usually, when one is active, the other is neglected. So, for example, you fall in love with someone, love is blind, and you throw caution to the wind and believe wholeheartedly in your new love. Two years later, the love of your life has betrayed you, you experience a serious loss of trust, and your skeptical identity rears its "show-me" head. Where has your "true believer" gone? Like a pendulum, your sense of self swings between the two. Sometimes, it becomes a dance in your relationship. When you're acting the trusting role, your partner is expressing the skeptical point of view. The next day the roles can switch.

The important thing to notice, when you're riding the pendulum, is that who you are is neither one side nor the other. You are neither the skeptic nor the true believer. You are an essence that goes beyond belief or doubt. It is that essence that is your core identity.

You can project the same pendulum on a guru, a priest, or any spiritual leader. Either you have absolute and true belief that he or she is perfect and can do no wrong, and everything he or she says is gospel, or you swing into the skeptical observer mode, detached, critical, looking for all the hypocrisy and incongruities in this self-professed master of the universe. Really, it is no different with a leader than a lover. If you set someone on a pedestal, you can rest assured that something will happen to cause your skeptic to reappear and make you doubt the object of your adoration.

Setting people up in this manner is quite popular in our culture, although the pattern of attacking leaders has always been prevalent. Nowadays, what with everyone's fifteen minutes of fame, we live in a perpetual cycle of worshipping the latest movie star, political leader, teenage rock star, cult hero, or New Age guru—only to relish in the scandals that inevitably follow such people and remind us of their humanity. It's as though by raising them up and then bringing them down we can say to ourselves, "They are no better than I." Of course, this is true, but we miss the point of our own greatness if we don't forgive and realize that even those surrounded by scandals occupy sacred ground in God's heart.

The true believer/skeptic dyad can reflect the progression of your perception of your parents. First, you see them as Gods. Not as expressions of God, but as real Gods. You place them on a pedestal and worship them. They can do no wrong. When you are a child and your father blasts you unjustly, you think it must be your fault because how can your father be wrong, or bad? Then, as you grow up, you notice that your parents are not perfect; they are human, not superhuman. They have their imperfections just like everyone else's parents. Suddenly, you knock them off the pedestal. You are a teenager, rebelling against authority, asserting your own. Of course, your disillusionment with your parents is ultimately as much an illusion as was your original fantasy. The circle is complete when you forgive your parents for being human and when you get to see them in the light of your forgiveness, which is the real light of God shining from within.

A parent can also transfer his own disillusionment with *his* parents to his children. Many people unknowingly are seeing their children through their unresolved emotions toward their parents. If you never recovered from the stage of disappointment, you may attract considerable disappointment into your family life as an adult. You may feel the need for your children to be the perfect beings your parents failed to be. This can apply a lot of pressure on your kids. After all, they need to feel as if they have room to fail, to be imperfect. How else can they learn and grow?

A perfectionist looks for perfection everywhere, but rarely finds it. He is obsessed with seeing all the little flaws in the world, then trying to correct them. If you are on a crusade for perfection, it can prevent you from experiencing the divinity in others. In your mind, God equals perfection, but people are never quite perfect enough, always disappointing in the long run, and so you are constantly moving from peaks to valleys in your emotional life. As I have mentioned before, the secret to understanding the universe is to realize that its flaws are part of its perfection. The second time around, God got it right. The perfectionist, however, doesn't quite see life this way. He tends to think that he could have done a better job than God, just as he could have done a better job than his father. For him, forgiveness is not the salvation of the world. Justice is.

❖ ❖ ❖ ❖

I asked the group to close their eyes and visualize the world. Imagine all the problems—poverty, pollution, hunger, hatred, drugs, disease, terrorism, and war. Feel compassion for the world, I suggested. After a few minutes I asked them to repeat the sentence "I forgive the world completely" several times. After the exercise, people shared. One woman stood up with tears in her eyes. "It was so beautiful. I could see the darkness of the world transform into light. It's as though all the problems are shadows cast by light."

❖ ❖ ❖ ❖

Try not to confuse the light of God with the particular vessel carrying it. It is very tempting to personalize God, especially when you first begin to see His light in others. You can easily transfer the source of this Light from the Creator to the Created. In other words, you can become a worshipper of human idols. You can find yourself spiritualizing and idealizing people whenever you see this Light shining from them. And, having found the Light in you, you can project it all over the place. So, while it is a tremendous experience to witness the Light of another being's sacred ground, it is important to remember that the Light is universal and not personal.

The Light is the whiteness of this page more than the words on it.

It can be a challenge to think of all humanity as family. God knows, there seems to be so much separating so many of us, what with historical, cultural, religious, and geographical differences. Moreover, even if we try to imagine that we are possibly all descended from one tree of life, or common ancestors, we have moved so far away from our common roots that it seems impossible to acknowledge the tree.

I think it is important and valuable to embrace humanity as one family, to see global conflicts as expanded family feuds. To do so shrinks the separation between us, and makes peace seems a little more attainable. I suggest that, if you cannot own common roots with all mankind, you at least attempt to adopt your humanity as your chosen family. If you think of the entire human race as your extended, mixed (yes, mixed-up, too) family, perhaps you will see a little more light in the world than otherwise.

We can adopt humanity as well as adapt to it. Imagine your inner sanctum mysteriously connected through a network of collective, unconscious caves to the sacred ground of every human being.

When you have a deep experience of your own sacred ground, you can extend this territory to include everyone. Knowing you are as God created you and knowing that others are as God created them enables you to accept people's flaws and understand they all have different histories, wounds, memories, and scars. Then, perhaps, you can open your heart and forgive them, knowing that the process of correction is part of God's perfect plan.

The City of Light is a city in constant renovation.

The Pitfall

The *pitfall* on Journey 8 is the temptation once again to see God outside oneself. If you fall into the trap of worshipping others at the expense of yourself, you are once again completely out of balance in your relationships to God, yourself, and others. Several years ago Mallie and I felt we were trapped in the guru trip. After working for eighteen years all around the world, we had built up a sizable spiritual community that tended to put us on a pedestal. We felt that, although we were aware of this collective projection, we could not stop it. Perhaps we had an unconscious need to be adored in some way, and so we were counter-transferring. Perhaps. In any case, we knew it was not working for us, and we believed it was not serving our followers either. So we stopped.

For two years we hardly led any seminars. We released our public life and took back our private lives. We let go of the personae that masked our real selves. It was an extremely enlightening and powerful transformation. When we did go back to work, we had purified ourselves from the dynamics of "hero worship" that had contaminated us. So, whether you are worshipping a lover, guru, saint, or master, *or* being worshipped by the masses, take stock of your soul. To love another more than you love yourself helps no one. To be worshipped by hordes but lose your private love is no better. In either situation it is time to be alone, enjoy your solitude, and remember who you are and who you are not.

Steps on the Eighth Journey

1. Don't let your inner sanctum be a hiding place.
2. When you have a conflict, look at the person in a new light.
3. Apologize when you behave inappropriately.
4. Think of yourself as a gatherer of light on your journey.
5. See every interaction as a holy encounter.
6. Try to recognize the light in others even when they misbehave.
7. Don't confuse the light of God with the particular container.
8. Talk to the essence of a person, not the personality.
9. Honor the souls of your parents and children.
10. Think of everyone as a messenger from God.
11. Have a sense of an extended, global family.

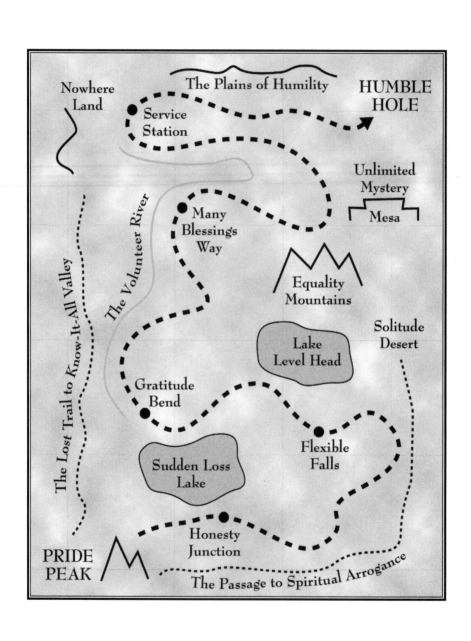

Journey 9

The Climb to Humility

As you approach home, your journey almost complete, it's hard not to be humbled by the vastness of the territory that surrounds you and fills you. You've crossed so many mountains and valleys, experiencing so much of your internal landscape. You've come to understand, learn, and know so many new things, but the mystery of all you don't know and will never know reminds you of the endlessness of the journey and the limitations that make you human. Thank God for all that is unknowable. It is this hidden aspect of the universe that keeps your curiosity alive, and your curiosity inspires you to new adventures, new mysteries, and new understanding.

To be humble is not to be lowly or defeated by life. On the contrary, it is the journey to the highest mountain peak, where your unobstructed view of Creation is overwhelming. You are uplifted by gratitude, and humbled by magnificence. In a state of unity and surrender, you arrive home to yourself, a straw mat greeting you with the words "Welcome Home" and a wooden sign offering the prayer "God Bless This House."

❖ ❖ ❖ ❖ ❖ ❖ ❖ ❖ ❖ ❖

I was teaching a seminar in Barcelona, Spain. I was feeling especially good about my work and full of myself. One of my favorites topics is *multiple intelligences,* and I was sharing with the group how they were all intelligent, only in different ways. Speaking very eloquently, and being blessed with an excellent translator, I looked out at the group and saw I was losing them. Suddenly, a voice inside my head said, "Tell them how stupid you are." I stopped in my tracks. I could feel my spiritual egotism resisting the suggestion, but I decided to go with it. I proceeded to share how stupid I am with languages. It's true. I work in many countries where English is not the primary language, and although I have been to these places many times I still need translators. So I confessed my stupidity, telling the group that it was important for me to know how stupid I was at language because it enabled me to find excellent translators, such as the one who was interpreting me right then and there. If I had to learn Spanish before I taught in a Spanish-speaking country, it might take many lifetimes.

The group understood me perfectly. And I was humbled by my own words.

THE CLIMB TO HUMILITY

The climb to humility begins as Pride Peak. There comes a point in most spiritual journeys where you think you've made it. You've arrived at enlightenment, you have the keys, and the gates are open for you. You can be in the middle of a meditation, transcending, feeling utter peace, and suddenly a voice inside your head whispers, "This is it," and you lose the whole experience. This is Pride Peak, where your ego pats your spirit on the back. Once you realize you're there, you can begin journeying again. Head for Honesty Junction and confess your flaws. Hopefully, you'll avoid Sudden Loss Lake and reach Flexible Falls without a lot of painful times. Eventually you'll move up to Gratitude Bend and Many Blessings Way, which will stir you to Service Station where you will do your good deeds on the Volunteer River. By the time you arrive at the great leveling Plains of Humility, you will have surrendered to the infinite mystery of the universe and the self-evident limitations of human knowledge.

Humility can be a tough bullet to bite, but we all bite it in good time, one way or the other. Journey 9 has no companion because it pertains both to you and others at the same time. Before we take a look at what humility really is, let's understand what it isn't. There have been many false notions of humility, and this is as good a time as any to dispel them.

False humility is the old belief that God is everything and you are nothing. You are an insignificant speck of dust in God's infinite grandeur. You amount to nothing of lasting value, and the best thing you can do with your worthless life is to lay it at the feet of God, Jesus, Buddha, Muhammad, or the Creator. Furthermore, you should be humble because humility is the opposite of pride and everyone knows what becomes of pride. To take pride in your successes rather than acknowledge God for your good fortune is both egotistical and blasphemous. Finally, humility is required in this life because we are all sinners and should bow our heads and pray for God's mercy and instant forgiveness.

God save us all from such myths about humility.

In many ways, humility seems like the very opposite of high self-esteem, especially when seen in the context of Western civilization in the twenty-first century. Most people believe that fame and fortune are where life's at, and if you can find your fifteen minutes of immortality you can end up sitting on top of the world. That's the goal, isn't it? To be on top of things, to be superior, to win at any cost, to kill the competition, to prevail. Recall Pearl Harbor, Hiroshima, Normandy. Think of the image of Nikita Khrushchev banging his shoe on a table at the UN, screaming, "We will bury you!" We don't have many good role models for humility in our world.

Of course, there's Gandhi, Nelson Mandela, Martin Luther King Jr., Mother Teresa, and many others whose strong sense of self blossomed in humble expression. But these people, while admired and respected for their historical achievements, hardly became inspirations for a generation of fortune hunters that worships the big bucks, Hollywood stars, mega-millionaire athletes, and Wall Street American dream catchers. In the Western mind, high self-esteem is more a function of taking pride in yourself than humbling yourself. It's an air of confidence, a personal magnetism, a charisma, a Rolex watch, an Armani suit, and a BMW.

The reason humility is so important in the development of true self-esteem is that, without it, we can stay stuck in spiritual egotism, a feeling of actual superiority because we know that God is in us. Of course, even humility can be dragged down into the world of ego. The ironic thing about humility is that once we think we have it, we don't. There is an ancient anonymous saying, "When we become aware of our humility, we've lost it." Once we advertise it, we become buffoons. Or, as Helen Nielson says, "Humility is like underwear; essential, but indecent if it shows."

Ted Turner jokes, "If I had any humility, I would be perfect."

GRATITUDE BEND

Stop for a moment and think of the things that have humbled you in your life. Maybe a time when you thought you had it all, but something happened to remind you otherwise. Maybe a time you lost a loved one, suffered a financial setback, or were confronted with physical illness. Think about how you felt at those times—sad, angry, afraid, hopeless? Now take a breath and try to see each occasion in the light of humility. Life humbled you. Each time life brings us to our knees, we have another opportunity to remember all we have to be grateful for, never to take it for granted, and see how delicate is the line between success and failure, love and loss, health and sickness. Find your humility in your blessings. Think of all you treasure in your life, the big things and the little things, and try never to take them for granted again.

Humility consists of many parts, one being gratitude. Developing an attitude of gratitude is a healthy choice in life. Usually, we are grateful for the good things and upset about the bad things. How many people have an expansive sense of gratitude, which includes life's lessons as well as life's more blatant gifts? Lessons are also valuable because, once learned, they teach us how to live more successfully. So we should try to be grateful for the stormy weather as well as the smooth sailing. But beyond that we also want to cultivate this attitude of gratitude for all of life. Every moment of existence, every piece of this living universe, is part of the miracle of Creation. When we are truly grateful, we are humbled by the awesomeness of life itself, and what that reflects about the Creator.

Another aspect of humility is honesty. It is obvious, but needs to be mentioned nonetheless, that a healthy sense of self entails honesty. The person who lies, conceals, hides secrets, and pretends is not really a person with high self-esteem. There is a huge difference between the man who walks down the street appearing to have confidence, power, and success at his disposal but who in reality is a fake, and the one who knows himself, likes himself, reveals himself, is vulnerable when appropriate, and discloses all. The first man might lie and cheat at his job, lie and cheat in his marriage, then walk tall with a great big false smile plastered on his face. The second man might say what he feels, have no hidden agenda, be all that he seems to be, and be trustworthy in all situations. One is a Great Pretender. The other is truly himself. One thinks he is bad but wears the mask of the good guy. The other knows he is good at heart and needs no mask to get by.

❖ ❖ ❖ ❖

Shirley was a lesson in humility. She was from New Jersey and her accent was shrill at times. Actually, always. Most of the other members of the group were quite cultured, many from Europe. Some of them would actually cringe at first when she opened her mouth. Of course, Shirley was not stupid, as she'd often remind you. "Do you think I'm stupid or something? You talk about love, but I can see that none of you like me." Or, "You talk about equality, but I can see you think you're better than me." She had a way of working the room. Playing the victim to the hilt, she would appeal to the guiltiest common denominator of the group, taking little responsibility even as she took up a great deal of space and time. If all else failed, she would admit that she had a tendency toward feeling victimized because her family were Holocaust victims, but, at the same time, she would do this in such a way as to make us feel that we must all be reincarnations of Nazis.

Shirley pushed all our buttons, and I was no exception. Since we were committed to a six-month journey in relationships, there was no avoiding Shirley as a valuable mirror we otherwise might have neglected. As time passed, one by one, the group began to warm up to her. Since she tended to hog the time for sharing, it was easy to see that she had needs she was committed to handling. When one person confronted her on her neediness, she replied, "Look, I may tick you off, but I paid good money to be in this program and I intend to get my money's worth."

In the next few months, everyone began to open up more and more. Shirley seemed to become an integral part of the group. But there was a wall separating her from the others. She knew it and most of us could feel it. Just when you thought you really loved her, she would turn on you. Once I was telling her that inside her sour exterior I could see a sweet little girl. "Yeah," she said, "and if I really reveal my sweetness, then you'd hurt me too."

"Maybe not," I replied.

"Maybe not." Shirley had been abandoned or abused so many times, her armor seemed to be cemented to her skin. And yet she had an honest and generous heart. If anyone needed support, be it a ride home, lunch money, or a shoulder to cry on, you could count on her.

One day a man in the group was moved by Shirley's tears. He tried to hug her, but she pushed him away.

"Don't come near me," she shouted. He was crushed. She could see it. "I feel so humiliated," she cried. And we felt so humbled by her mountains of pain and valleys of sorrow. Shirley knew how to go for it, however, and in the end she helped us all climb that trail of humility so that we could claim our honesty and humanity more deeply.

Although assertive, aggressive, and sometimes obnoxious, Shirley was somehow a barometer of the group's commitment to itself. In learning how to release their judgments of her, the group not only learned tolerance, they learned to be humbled by their own hidden needs for attention, as well as their fears of not being accepted when they expressed themselves fully. They went deeper into their own vulnerability and emerged stronger for having done so.

One of Shirley's favorite lines, which she used both to reveal and conceal herself, was, "I know you think I'm arrogant, but who isn't?"

Near the end of the program, after many members shared their love and appreciation for her, Shirley sobbed as we'd never seen her. "I know you mean what you're saying, but it's still so hard for me to receive it. I'm so afraid you'll abandon me once the group is finished."

One by one, each person shared they felt the exact same way. We all sat in silence, a circle of unbroken tenderness.

Full disclosure is a rare phenomenon in today's world.

Once, I was giving a small seminar for advanced students in Caracas, Venezuela. The topic was Intimacy and Intrigue. At a certain point I was discussing the importance of honesty in a loving relationship, how a committed relationship was predicated on both people having nothing to hide, keeping no secrets, and putting all their cards on the table. I distinguished this from the old paradigm where a man might have a secret mistress, or affairs, or a woman might gossip negatively to her girlfriends behind her man's back. As I was talking, a man in the back of the room became agitated. It just so happened he was a psychologist who had a different point of view. He shared that it could be dangerous to tell all to a mate. You could hurt her feelings, cause her great grief. When I pointed out that I understood what he was feeling and I had been there, done that, what I discovered is that underneath my fear of hurting my mate was my deeper fear that she would hurt me, or even leave me. So my secrecy was my selfishness, not my compassion. Besides, if your partner cannot accept you as you are, perfect yet imperfect, can you really say she is the right person for you? Your partner should be your best friend, someone who knows everything about you and loves you nonetheless.

The honest person is humble because he doesn't fly his honesty like a flag. He knows it doesn't make him better than the next person. It just makes him more honest about his shortcomings. From such a space, he can work on self-improvement without comparing himself to the next person. This sets the stage for a life of integrity, another factor in humility. When you walk your talk and talk your walk, you live an integrated life. Of course, we don't all do this all the time. I would be lying to you if I said I always live up to my ideals. I don't. That's why they are called ideals. They are principles to be striven toward, visions to be realized, and dreams to wake up to. But we are all in the process of living up to our ideals, which is why we should not criticize others when we see them stumble. When my brother stumbles, I see my own frailty. And I offer a helping hand. Your integrity rests in your honesty, humility, and commitment to your higher self. Once again, integrity is not an excuse for false superiority so much as a reason for compassion.

Humility without compassion is like love without generosity. Such humility is a pose rather than a passion. Many people mistake their guilt for compassion. When you think you are hurting others and you feel responsible for other people's pain, then your desire to help is motivated by a need to pay off your feelings of guilt. Many people, for example, give to charities for the wrong reasons. One such reason is obviously the tax benefit you receive. But a deeper motivation might be your guilt for having more than others, or feeling responsible because you think that when you win, others necessarily lose. Therefore your success causes the failure of others, and you should give them a hand.

While falsely motivated charity is better than no charity, true charity is based on seeing no separation between yourself and the needy. You are not guilty when you look at a beggar. You are not responsible for his plight in life. However, what you *are* responsible for is giving back to the whole, which in turn supports you. What you *are* responsible for is extending a helping hand because the hand that you help helps you. When someone is down and you offer a hand to raise him up, once he is risen there are two of you to continue the journey. Your team grows in size. Your extended love is more powerful than your withheld love. Charity is an act of humility because you know when you see someone destitute that "there, but for the grace of God, go I." Charity acknowledges the interconnectedness of the human family and the commitment to the whole, not just your own part.

When I was in Brazil, I was surprised that instead of saying "thank you" or "gracias," they say "obrigado" (for "much obliged"). There is a difference between expressing gratitude and a feeling of indebtedness. If you feel you are obligated to everyone in this sense—to your parents, your children, your brothers and sisters, and the world—you will probably resent this feeling of entrapment. When a mother says to her first-born child, "You *should* share your baseball bat with your little brother," that *should* becomes an obligation in the negative sense. She could phrase her suggestion differently. "I bet your brother would love it if you showed him how to swing that bat."

There is another way, a higher way, in which we are all obligated to each other. We are obligated because we belong to one planet, one biosystem, one human family. We are obligated to give back to the planet, the family, and everyone because when we replenish the whole, we personally benefit. When the air is clean and the seas are pure, we all win. When poor countries become wealthy, there is more for everyone. And when we give to our brothers and sisters, our brothers and sisters have more to give to us. This kind of obligation, which encompasses social responsibility, is simply an expression of seeing the big picture.

True charity begins at home. If you are not generous to those you live with, what does it matter if you are a great benefactor to the world? Generosity can take many forms: financial, emotional, intellectual, spiritual. When you give from your heart, you are being generous. When you are kind, you are being generous. When you genuinely care about someone, you are being generous. Don't be afraid to give. Avoid the temptation to think you will lose what you have if you give. Think of giving as a way to prime the pump for your own success. Sometimes I suggest to people that they keep a "generosity generator" in their house. This can be a glass jar, cigar box, or any container. You use it to stash away extra money—bills and coins. Whenever it is full, give it away. Walk down the street being generous to the needy. Or give it to your friends, family, people at work, complete strangers. Make sure you are not giving to manipulate, seduce, or obligate others to be in your debt. Practice random acts of generosity and kindness. Notice how good you feel when you give in this spirit.

The power of humility is enormous. You can move mountains if you respect the obstacles and honor the challenge. If you don't respect the opposition, you cannot have lasting success and satisfaction. For example, good sportsmanship, something that is lacking in many competitive sports these days, is based on humility: respect for the opponent. Nowadays, you see professional athletes taunting the other team, flaunting their own success, insulting the dignity of the opponent. Even young children in organized sports are learning to show off their success, posing obnoxiously, performing victory celebrations far beyond good taste. You see the parents of youngsters just getting started in sports screaming madly, taking out their own frustrations on a Little League team or even a Pee Wee league.

I heard a story recently about something that happened at a kids' ice hockey game—young kids. The puck hit one boy in the face and play was stopped, as is the custom. All the kids dropped to a knee and waited. The kid who hit the puck was concerned and approached the young player on the ice. His mother, in the stands, started screaming for him to shoot the puck into the open net. "Shoot, shoot!" she screamed as an eight-year-old lay bleeding on the ice.

It concerns me that we live in a society where people have forgotten the meaning of competition. It's not about winning and losing. It's not about burying the competition. When one team wins and the other loses, the winning team should honor and respect the other team. They should praise their opponents for bringing out the best in them. And never should they believe that winning a mere game makes them superior in any significant way to the team on whose backs they climbed to success. Be grateful to the one you defeat because, without him, you would have won nothing, achieved nothing, and excelled at nothing.

We need to learn how to be humble in victory and proud in defeat. For surely, in sports as in life, what goes around comes around.

Sometimes I think of humility as flexibility. Where I live there are old pine trees stretching high to the sky. They are big, strong. Many of them have lived far longer than I. When a storm comes and the wind blows, I see them bend, wave, sway, but they rarely break. When the snow falls—and sometimes a lot of snow falls—I observe their limbs grow heavy with the white weight. They droop, sag, bend, but they rarely crack. Trees are flexible. It is one of the secrets of their power and longevity. So is a blade of grass. In life, flexibility can be a great asset whereas intransigence can be a problem. Being humble is knowing when to bend, how to bend, and why bending is sometimes preferred to stiffening.

The great leaders knew this. Gandhi built his philosophy of passive resistance on the concept of bending but not breaking. Today we don't like that word *passive*. We think aggression is the key to success and victory. But aggression breeds aggression. Defensiveness invites attack. The more we build weapons, the more we use them. The more we build guns, the more our children kill each other. In *A Course in Miracles* we are told "In my defenselessness my safety rests." This idea is insane to the ego. The ego is defined as a healthy system of self-protection and defense. As a nation must defend itself, an individual enjoys the right to bear arms. Yet, think about it. Think of all the literal arms that have been lost by the right to bear arms. Think of all the dead soldiers, innocent civilians, women and children who have been sacrificed.

◇ ◇ ◇ ◇

When you give up your personal defense system, you become more powerful because you experience the power of humility. The power of flexibility. If you are attacked, you can turn the other cheek. You can be still. You can take a breath. You can wait. Because without a reactive response, the attacker cannot fight you. When there is a tug of war with a piece of rope, if one side releases the rope, it wins. To give up the fight is to win. If your body is not used as a weapon, then your spirit stands strong. This is why civil protests can end a war, change a nation, and challenge prejudice and bigotry more than aggressive protests. If you don't like the words *passive resistance,* think of it as the power of humility. It can overcome even the worst of times, not to mention the temptations you face when you're sitting on top of the world.

In a relationship, it is the same as out in the world. If you and your partner are at war, if you are in opposition, who will give up the fight first? Of course, your ego will always tell you that if you stop fighting, you lose. In reality, if you keep fighting, you will both inevitably lose something really important, more important than the issue of your fight—you will lose each other. So who has the guts, the wisdom, and the humility to say, "no more"? In my relationship with Mallie, we return to one thought over and over: "I'd rather win love than arguments." Love is salvation. War is hell.

◇ ◇ ◇ ◇

When Oscar Wilde arrived in America, he told Customs, "I have nothing to declare but my genius!" Hardly a humble remark, yet somehow honest. Albert Einstein, who never declared his own genius and was always humbled by the mystery of Creation, said, "What I see in Nature is a magnificent structure that we can comprehend only very imperfectly, and that must fill a thinking person with a feeling of humility." Einstein and Buddha shared a sense of cosmic humility. They both perceived the universe as created from an endless void. When we think of a universe created out of nothingness, how can we not be impressed and humbled by the vastness of it all? But if all matter, energy, molecules are no more than compressed emptiness, are we not all created out of that same void? So when you feel as if you are nothing, let it be an invitation to humility rather than a sign of low self-esteem. You can be nothing, in the sense of worthless. Or you can be nothing, in the sense of cosmic.

Remember, even the greatest men and women are made of the same emptiness as you. The key is never to confuse your quantum humility with a low opinion of yourself. Be humbled by your genius, beauty, and magnificence. And know that, although you are a part of the emptiness, alone in solitude, you are also a part of the whole, connected to everything that exists, past, present, and future. *It is one of the divine contradictions of life that you are alone and yet all One at the same time.*

Einstein also said, "Only a life lived for others is a life worthwhile." By this he did not mean you should sacrifice for others. But he was touching on an important aspect of humility, namely service. The concept of service is a popular one nowadays. Almost every business has a customer service department, and it is widely recognized that the quality of service can often be the only distinguishing quality between one product and another. However, there is a huge difference between service as a self-serving function of business and serving humanity from a foundation of love, compassion, and humility.

When you experience humility, you naturally want to place your life in the service of humanity. You feel your compassion and you want to help people. God knows, we all need help, but some more than others. When you think of all the hungry, homeless, and sick people on this planet, it is overwhelming. What can one person do? But we all must do everything possible. It is necessary that we reach deep into our hearts, if not our pockets, and find our own way of contributing to the larger community. Some people do volunteer work. Others devote their careers to serving humanity. Whether you adopt a child, save the whales, walk for AIDS, donate blood—do something.

Service is not servitude. I am not suggesting that you become a servant. To serve is to be of use, to share your value with others to improve the quality of life on the planet. Of course, there are times when we all find ourselves in actual positions of service. You find yourself at a job where you are called on to serve others. You're a waitress, a bank teller, a salesperson, or working in customer service. When God puts you in such a position, it is an opportunity to master humility and service. If you remember that the customer comes first and that your job is to satisfy the customer, then you can experience the spiritual satisfaction of placing your energy in the service of others. Far too often people in service positions resent what they are doing, take it out on the customer or client, and daydream about doing what they really would like. This is unfortunate because when you have the opportunity to make a difference in someone else's life, you should take advantage of it. When God says to help someone, He is acknowledging your value and usefulness to humanity. And nobody appears at your doorstep in need who has not been sent by God.

SERVICE STATION

Devote yourself to service. Take a boat down the Volunteer River. Give back to Creation because you are grateful and want to improve the quality of life around you. Think of one form of service that would bring joy to your heart and help others. Perhaps you want to mentor a child, or offer aid to the elderly, the blind, the homeless. Or maybe you're drawn to hospice work for the terminally ill. Whatever grabs your heart, do it. And do it from a space of gentle kindness, without calling attention to yourself. Let your presence be a healing force in somebody's life.

In a sense, humility is the recognition that there is a wheel of fortune that turns our lives. It is the understanding that, to live a life in balance and harmony, it is both practical and wise never to get too excited when fortune is smiling on you and never to get too depressed when fortune frowns on you. Whether you are on top of the wheel or at the bottom, the wheel is turning, your fortunes are always in the process of changing, and being comfortable with the wheel is being comfortable with life. Even when the wheel feels more like a roller coaster.

People win and lose fortunes every day. Nowadays, with the stock market as it is, you can become a multimillionaire overnight, and lose it all by the next evening. If your self-esteem is rooted in the fluctuations of your financial fortune, you will be in for a rocky ride. If you know who you are and what your real value is, regardless of the ups and downs of your finances, you can play the money game from a detached, humble, and calm point of view. Your whole life does not depend on what number appears on the board when the bell rings. You know that the successful man is not necessarily the one who dies with the most toys.

You know that all the money in the world is but a drop in the bucket of the infinite emptiness that contains us all.

◇ ◇ ◇ ◇

Once upon a time there was a very wealthy man. In fact, he was the richest man in the community. His name was Simon. People from all over the world came to see Simon, hoping to do business with him or at least rub shoulders with him. Simon was very cautious with his wealth. He never gave to charities or beggars, claiming they had to learn to fend for themselves. He was very shrewd and would only do business with others if he was clear that it would benefit him directly. He even denied his own family his wealth, giving his wife and three sons only the bare minimum to survive. All over the kingdom Simon was known for his frugality and stinginess. Although he seemed to have everything in the world, there was one thing Simon lacked and that was humility. For Simon the word was a joke. "Why should I be humble?" he declared. "I'm the richest man on earth!"

Late one night a stranger came knocking on Simon's door. A servant opened the door and saw the stranger dressed in rags. "What do you want, beggar?" he asked, somewhat disgusted. The stranger said he didn't want anything, but he had an important message for Simon and must speak to him immediately. The servant was ready to shut the door when the stranger handed him a gold coin. Looking at the coin, then at the stranger, the servant noticed an unusual light glowing in the stranger's eyes. So he told him to wait. Some time passed and Simon came to the door, irritated by this intrusion. "What's so important that a beggar like you wakes a man like me at this ungodly hour?" The stranger smiled and asked if he could enter. Somehow, Simon couldn't refuse and so the stranger entered. They sat down together and drank some hot tea. The stranger told Simon he was a messenger, nothing more. When Simon asked whom the message was from, the stranger ignored the question and simply said, "The message is this: if you don't give all your wealth away within twenty-four hours, you will lose everything." Simon stared at the stranger, not believing what he had heard. He noticed a bright radiance deep inside the stranger's eyes. The stranger smiled and placed a hand on Simon's heart. "Take heart," he said. "Do not fear." But Simon became very scared, even though he didn't show it. He laughed abruptly and too loud, and, giving the stranger a bag full of coins—in itself a strange act for Simon—he showed him to the door.

The next morning Simon told his wife about the stranger. "What will you do?" she asked, but Simon had no answer. "If you give away everything, you will have nothing. But if you don't, you might lose everything." Simon smiled at the irony. He left the house feeling like a different person. He didn't know why, but suddenly he was seeing everything differently. He no longer felt that old greed tightening his muscles. When he saw a beggar sitting on the street, he stopped. Tears came to his eyes. He offered a hand and helped the man to his feet. He removed a bag of gold coins and handed it to the beggar. Later, when Simon was in his office, visitors from all over the kingdom came, begging for contributions. One woman wanted money for a new school. A group of businessmen wanted to construct a new marketplace. An organization wanted free housing for the poor. A man wanted to build a new theater. Another man had a vision for a new temple. And another wanted to build a new hospital. Simon was terribly moved by each of their stories. He gave them all what they asked for. By the end of the day, Simon had given all his money away. As he was walking home, he began to laugh. He felt so lighthearted. Somehow he felt richer with no money than he had when he was wealthy. As he walked, he saw the stranger approaching from the distance. Simon stopped him, but the stranger did not seem to recognize him. "Excuse me, but I am blind," said the stranger. Simon began to cry for this man. He reached into his pockets, but he had nothing left to give except the keys to his house. So he gave away the keys to his house. The stranger thanked him. The next day Simon, his wife, and his three boys walked out of town with packs on their backs. When they reached the gates of the city, the stranger was standing there. "Where are you going, Simon?" he asked. "I don't know, but I must leave. There is nothing for me here. I have nothing." The stranger smiled and waved his hand at the city. "Are you blind, Simon. Look." And Simon looked back at the city, but it was all new. There were new buildings, hospitals, theaters, schools, temples. Simon was extremely moved by the miraculous transformation he now saw. His heart was full of love for his city and he cried at the thought of leaving. "You have everything, Simon. All that you have given is yours. Come home." Simon still didn't understand. "But I *have* no home. The home that I had is your home now." Putting an arm around Simon, the stranger whispered to him, "Yes, my friend, and my home is your home as well."

The Pitfall

The *pitfall* on the rise to humility is the martyr trip. It would be a shame if, after climbing all the way up the ladder of self-development, you suddenly fell off and tumbled back into self-denial and self-sacrifice. You don't want to mistake humility for a life of abstinence and self-neglect, thinking you have to sacrifice yourself to gain God's love. You don't want to see your life as a punishment but, rather, as a reward. It is important that your humility bring you to service from a sense of fullness and gratitude for life. You are so much in love with your life that you want to share this high state of being with the world. You have developed a strong sense of self, and, knowing who you are, you freely choose to devote yourself to the improvement of the world. Knowing who you are, you want everyone to have the same opportunity, the same knowledge, the same joy. You want all the children of the world to have a fair opportunity to reach their full potential in this lifetime so that they, in turn, can help make this world a better place for their children. You are humbled by the task ahead. But you have the courage to take action. You are clear, and therefore you no longer confuse a life of humility, devotion, and service with a life of martyrdom.

Steps on the Ninth Journey

1. Don't get too excited by the peaks or too depressed by the valleys.
2. Think of the unlimited mystery of the universe.
3. It's okay to know you don't know.
4. When you lose someone, be grateful for the times you shared.
5. When times are hard, keep your sense of humor.
6. Be honest about your shortcomings.
7. Be flexible.
8. When you fail, remember you're still the same person.
9. It's good enough to be a human being.
10. Do volunteer work.
11. You're equal to the one you look up to and the one you look down upon.

Epilogue

Where is home? What does *home* mean? It has been said that "Home is where your heart is," which would imply, on the one hand, that home lies within your body, the physical place where you dwell, and on the other hand, that home is wherever your heart may wander.

Of course, home is primarily thought of as a place where family gathers. In this sense, your home might be where you lived as a child and grew up toward adulthood. Perhaps it's where you still live, or where your parents live. Some people never wander very far from home. Many always consider their parents' home their real "home" and not until they die do the children become the full owners of their own home. In Europe, people frequently live near their parents, more so than in the USA where we tend to drift further and further away from our place of origin. Our birth home.

Home implies father and mother, brother and sister. Your home consists of those relationships that bind you under one roof in one family. You may have run away from one or more of those relationships, but until you heal what made you run in the first place you will never experience yourself as truly at home.

"Make yourself at home" is a common greeting, sometimes sincere, sometimes empty. If your birth home was a frightful experience, the thought of making yourself at home might cause your feet to itch. How can you be comfortable in any home until the very notion of home implies a certain level of peace, safety, and support? How can you be at home in your own body if you've suffered such trauma that you needed to disconnect from your own body to survive emotionally? And, finally, how can you relate to Earth as your home planet if your soul is secretly seeking another universe altogether?

"Welcome home," we are told. But if we never felt welcome in our own families in the first place—if we felt we never belonged—all the other "welcome homes" we hear resonate to the emptiness and loneliness of our original entry into this world.

This book has been about journeying home, which in a sense is a contradiction. Usually, we think of a journey as moving away from home toward some new, exciting territory—an adventure in a foreign kingdom. Sometimes a journey is by foot, by car, by air, or by boat. Some people journey in groups, some alone. Some take familiar tours, others "the road less traveled." In all cases, however, coming home is usually thought of as the mere completion of the journey, the return to a familiar starting place.

I have a hat with the following statement on it: "Life is a journey, not a guided tour."

A spiritual journey, however, has its own curious landscape and topography.

A journey of spirit leads us to a home that has neither walls nor windows (although you may discover some closets, basements, and attics)—a home that welcomes all to the dinner table, embracing humanity as kin, but that nevertheless resides in some mysterious inner sanctum requiring personal keys for access. A journey of the soul is about neither the isolation of the hermit/monk nor the politics of relationships so much as about the awareness of both solitude and connection. Such a trip is an opening of the heart within the home of our body, true, but it is also an external extension into the family of man. In the end, nobody can come home to himself by himself. All who take this journey take mankind with them, as mankind itself takes them with it. And so, these nine journeys home are aspects of what I call *collective self-esteem.*

We all have our roots and our routes in this life. Your roots might have been more painful than mine, or vice versa. And my routes might be more circuitous than yours, or not. In either case, the journey home to self-esteem is a journey of forgiveness and compassion, which begins with yourself and stretches to include others, one by one in every sacred encounter. As you extend yourself to include the strangers you meet on your journey and as you open your heart to embrace those you previously shut out, your soul grows and glows in greater light.

In this book I have described nine journeys to lead you to the promised land, which is both an internal kingdom and an external world. These are journeys from rejection to acceptance, fear to tolerance, resentment to gratitude, pride to humility. They are journeys that are healing and revealing, requiring recovery and discovery, and climbing up to the summit of your own divine magnificence. But in the end, the journey home is a humbling experience because you confront all your own imperfections along the way, which allows you to feel compassion for all humanity.

Finally, you come home to your spiritual roots, to the Source, the Creator. To this place of wonder and awe, the home you have always dreamed of, you bring the light you have collected on the path. Here you feel welcome as never before. Here you feel united with all those souls who came before you and all those yet to come. Here you are forever cradled in the arms of God's love. You have completed the journey from home to home.

About My Work

My work consists of facilitating rebirthing sessions, seminars, and talks to students, teachers, and parents. I have been a rebirther since 1976 and am one of the twelve original certified rebirthers in the world. Rebirthing is a healing process that uses the breath as a vehicle to regress to early memories, release trauma, and recover from the damage done to your developing sense of self. Although a gentle technique, it can be very powerful and empowering as an experience. Together with Mallie, I am the founder of ISLP, International Seminars Leadership Programs, which offers training programs for beginning, intermediate, and advanced students in the international rebirthing community. We offer weekend seminars around the world in relationships and rebirthing, and in Connecticut we present our advanced programs every summer. In 1998 I was moved to begin the International Self-Esteem Project, whose mission is to help raise the self-esteem of children and adults throughout the world. I am available for talks with classes, teachers, and parents, as well as for media appearances. To find out more about my work, visit my website at www.bobmandel.com; email me at rmandel@snet.net; call me at 860-868-9153; or write to me at:

ISLP
21 Sabbaday Lane
Washington, CT 06793

Finally

Hold Your Children

Aretha Salter, founder of the Aware Parenting Institute, has many interesting stories and studies about the value of holding a child. Here is one of them:

In the eighteenth century the enlightened despot Frederick the Great, King of Prussia, had an interesting idea. He wondered what would happen if he brought a hundred newborn babies together from different countries and raised them in one space under exactly the same conditions. In particular, he was curious whether, if nobody ever spoke to them or had any contact with them, they would evolve a universal language among themselves. So, being king, he proceeded with his experiment.

How can we help the children? This is a question that resonates in my mind daily. One of the driving forces behind the International Self-Esteem Project is the desire to support children in loving themselves and others. How troublesome it is to witness children shooting other children, shooting up, and obsessed by electronic images so violent in their content that if you ever dreamed such things you would wake up screaming in the middle of the night. How upsetting to notice the increase in teenage drugs, unprotected sex, pregnancy, abortion, and, yes, suicide! Our children, the future of the world, are crying out for help. How can we turn things around?

Several years back two clients came to me, two adults, mother and daughter. I worked with the daughter first, who was in her thirties, a wonderful lady who was a force in her community and a beloved friend to many. In her session she regressed to different times in her life when she had felt abused or rejected, beginning with her birth. When she was born, she told me, her mother rejected her completely. "It was no big deal," she laughed bitterly. "That's the way it was in my family. If you were a girl, you were unwanted." She brushed this aside as though it really didn't amount to much, telling me how she had overcome all this rejection through therapy and self-help. She reminded me of my idea of a *rejection quota,* assuring me that she had fulfilled hers very early in life. At the end of the session, when I asked her how her relationship was with her mother, she told me it was great except that her mother loved her too much these days.

Next I worked with the mother, who was a powerful, middle-aged woman ridden with guilt. She lay down and began to relax into her breathing, but almost immediately began to talk about the birth of her daughter. She told me how throughout the pregnancy she prayed every day that she would have a son. When she gave birth to a girl, she was devastated, she told me. "It was more like a funeral than a birth for me." She refused to touch the child for three days. She wanted it to die. I have heard many stories of unwanted children, but this was one of the heaviest, I assure you. Finally, when I asked her why it was so horrible to have a girl, she laughed, the same cynical giggle as her daughter. She went on to tell me that she came from a long line of unwanted women and that when she herself was born her mother had rejected her the same way. I asked her how she felt about that and whether she could ever forgive her mother. "What's to forgive?" she replied, "I agree with her totally."

If we want to help our children, we have to forgive our parents. It's that simple. What's unresolved in you toward your parents gets transmitted to your children.

One scene I see repeated far too many times is the scene where a parent, furious at a child, is screaming at that little person with the full force of all his rage. I see a little body shaking in fear at the very magnitude of the energy being dumped on her. Or I see the child zoning out, knowing that the only way to deal with abuse is to skip town, as it were. Either way, I just wish I could go over to that child, hold her close to me, and say something reassuring.

I have witnessed the following scene more than once. A mother has the belief that nobody listens to her. As a child her perception, true or false, was that adults did not hear what she was saying. When she grew up, she continued to experience the consequences of her perception. Her parents still do not listen to her. Her husband doesn't either. And her children seem to be deaf, or so she says. In addition, she has shifted the idea of not being listened to so that it now means she is not being obeyed. If people listened to her, they would do what she is telling them to do because obviously it is the right thing to do. The endgame of this pattern is that the mother is screaming so loudly at her children that they cannot possibly hear what she is saying. Moreover, they tune out, disassociate, roll their eyes, and wait for the onslaught to pass. After she vents her frustration, the mother roars at whoever happens to be in the vicinity, "You see what I mean? Nobody ever listens to me!"

I was brought up, like many of you, by parents who believe in the "do as I say, not as I do" philosophy. So, when I was screamed at, I was supposed to ignore the rage and listen to the words, a tough task for any adult let alone a kid who is so sensitive to adult energy swings. I could never do it. The only thing I ever learned from adults who vented their anger, frustration, and resentment on me was that I never wanted to scream like that when I grew up. I also developed the habit of not being able to listen when I was blasted with someone else's rage.

Lucy told me the following story. When her two daughters were young, they would act out in the supermarket. They would begin to argue with each other, escalating into a full fight, and then sit down in an aisle screaming at the top of their lungs. Poor Lucy was totally embarrassed. What could she do? She felt totally helpless, at wit's end. And this scene occurred over and over again. Finally, she had a major realization. She realized that she was stuffing her own anger and, in fact, had a lifelong pattern of repressing her anger, which originated in her relationship with her own mother. The next time Lucy took the girls to the supermarket and they sat in the aisle in their temper tantrum, Lucy did the same thing. She sat down, pounded the floor, pulled at her hair, and screamed as loudly as she could how much she hated going to the market! Immediately, the two girls stopped screaming. They came to their mother and began to laugh. Then Lucy began to laugh. And, in their laughter, something was resolved because there was never another incident in the supermarket. While I generally do not recommend that parents "act out" in such a manner, I share this story with you as an example of children acting out the unresolved emotions of their parents.

King Frederick gathered his hundred orphan babies and locked them in a large room. He made sure they were well provided for in terms of food, clothing, and other basics. The only thing he insisted on was that they have no interaction with any adult since that would spoil the premise of the experiment. Their immediate needs were attended to, but they had no emotional contact. Nobody talked to them. Nobody touched them with tenderness. Frederick waited patiently to see what language they would finally speak.

Who are our children? Who are these amazing beings with small bodies and little or no vocabulary? Are they less than adults because they have less weight and fewer words (if more brain cells)? Of course not. A child is, in every significant aspect, equal to an adult, and deserving of the same respect. When a parent disapproves of a child and that child shuts down because he can do little else, given his physical and verbal limitations, the result can be devastating. The child internalizes the abuse and somehow waits for the day when he is big enough and has a loud enough voice to terrorize someone else, such as his own child. The *might makes right* mindset and behavior are successfully transplanted to another body. Is this the family tradition we want to pass down to the next generation? I doubt it.

Parents often squelch their child's self-esteem. If the parents don't have high self-esteem, they can even feel threatened by a child expressing his. How many times have you seen a child having a wonderful time, expressing his sense of joy, play, and creativity only to be disapproved of by a repressed parent or teacher.

"Keep it down, kids!"

"Pipe down in there!"

"Lower your voices!"

"Do you need a time-out?"

"I'm warning you for the last time!"

I have often seen adults cringing in their seats when in the presence of happy, enthusiastic children. Why are they so embarrassed by such a natural display of joy and exuberance? Shouldn't their own spirits be uplifted by the energy? The problem is, the behavior does not compute with their own upbringing. Children should be seen and not heard, right? What's *that* all about?

Talk to your children from your heart. Listen to them when they speak from *their* hearts. Have meals together. Read to them. Create a family ritual in which everyone can participate. Kiss your children. Tuck them in when they are ready for bed. Massage their little bodies. Hold them tight when they need it. Don't point fingers at them. Always say "I love you" at the end of each day. And each morning begin the new day with those same magical words. Don't think of your child's needs as an endless string of chores for you. What your child needs, spiritually as well as physically, is also what nurtures you. The bond goes two ways. When you see raising a child as a way to (1) witness and influence the development of a beautiful soul, (2) dance with your own inner child, and (3) make peace with your own parents, you realize what a gift you have been given. What a gift and what a challenge! And what a responsibility as well.

I was once in a classroom of twenty nine-year-olds, a teacher, and a teacher's aide. Nancy, the teacher, is a friend of mine, and she had invited me to talk to her class about self-esteem. I talked for a few minutes, then asked the kids how they felt about self-esteem. Naomi was eager to tell me that she really liked herself. She was bubbling with energy, enthusiasm, and innocence. She shared how she was a really good math student, a good singer, and a wonderful older sister. All the other kids agreed. "It's true," one said. "Naomi's the best artist, too," added another. Naomi took me by the hand and showed me some drawings she had done. It was after September 11 and there was a drawing of the two Trade Towers being buried in a coffin. The towers were holding hands. The teacher's aide was getting uncomfortable and said to Naomi that someone else might want to share, too. Naomi replied that she wanted me to see a photograph she took of her little brother. The aide said, "Not now." Nancy intervened and said it was okay. We had time. The aide excused herself and left the room.

Of course, different people would have different reactions to a child displaying self-esteem in such a manner. A parent with low self-esteem would be embarrassed by his own child's exuberant behavior, attempt to suppress it, apologize for it, and maybe even punish the child for "showing off," as it were. It always seemed a little absurd to me that we go to school and learn "show and tell," but then there's this other thing called "showing off," which we are supposed to avoid.

For a child to show off how good he feels is wonderful. Of course, if it is done in a negative way that is both competitive and diminishing of others, then that's another story. In such a case, a parent can gently remind a child that it is wonderful to acknowledge oneself, but not at the expense of others. More often than not, however, the problem rests in the fact that the child's natural tendency to love himself is in conflict with the parent's repressive conditioning. In other words, the parent unconsciously imitates his own parent in disapproving of his child's self-expression, thereby both expressing his own resentment, misplaced though it is, and being the good child following the way of his parents.

The worst cases are ones of abuse. When a parent strikes, spanks, or beats a child, it is a crime of the heart. Usually, this type of behavior springs spontaneously from a frustrated parent who, as a last resort, follows his own parents' example of "tough love." Most of the time, the parent is not even aware that he is being abusive when he is physically violent. It is a sad statistic that abused children frequently grow up to abuse their own children.

Research tells us that children brought up with excessive discipline, restrictions, and punishment tend to grow into more troubled, less productive adults. On the other hand, the solution is not to be a permissive parent who lacks boundaries, rules, and guidelines. Children need to learn limits. At the same time, their unlimited potential must be respected. An experiment regarding food is a good example. Two groups of children were given different dietary options. The first group was told they had to eat their vegetables, vitamins, fruit, protein. And no junk food! The second group was allowed to eat anything they wanted. Within a very short period of time, the first group rebelled and ate junk food while the second group gravitated toward a healthy, well-balanced diet.

We must respect the souls of our children. You have a right to be you. And they have a right to be them!

When a child does something "bad," see it as a learning opportunity rather than time for punishment. Teach the child that her behavior is inappropriate to the wonderful person she is. Find out what motivated her to behave in a negative way. See if she is looking for negative attention because she isn't getting enough positive attention. Try to show her that she can take responsibility for her behavior without feelings of guilt! Don't tell her, "You should know better!" But talk to the part of her that does know better. When a parent does this homework with his child, the child is much less subject to peer pressure toward negative behavior. Most of all, you want to encourage your child to express herself, her feelings, her thoughts, her joy and playfulness. Listen carefully to what she is really saying, asking for, and upset about. The more you allow your child to be her whole and wonderful self at home, the more she will both know that self and express that self wherever she goes in the world and in her life!

The more a parent empowers his child, the more the child flourishes, especially if the parent is on the path toward healing his own childhood wounds.

Several years ago a wise, witty, and wonderful woman, Vanessa, enrolled in a long-term program. Vanessa was forty-two and desperately wanted to be pregnant. She and her partner had been trying unsuccessfully for many months. We were a small group of twelve who met for one weekend a month for nine consecutive months. Every month Vanessa would report on her progress, hoping that her personal healing process would somehow enable her to carry a fertilized egg.

One weekend, the group was sharing about abortions when Vanessa, a large woman, revealed an interesting piece of her personal history. When she was eighteen, while in college, she became pregnant. She never told anyone.

She was terrified that her mother, a very prominent member of the community, would be shamed by this illegitimate child. When it was time to give birth, Vanessa went into the bathroom in her single dorm room and delivered the baby by herself. Then she wrapped the baby tight and left it outside on the doorstep. The next morning, when the baby was discovered, Vanessa pretended to be as surprised as everyone else.

Vanessa said she had never told this story to anyone before. I felt there was a connection between this event and her inability to conceive a child now. I sensed that a part of Vanessa was stuck in not wanting to show a pregnancy for fear of her mother's response. I suggested she write a letter to her mother telling the complete truth. Although reluctant, she agreed to do it. At our next meeting she read aloud a very moving letter to her mother. She sent it off. Soon after, Vanessa became pregnant. She now has an adorable set of twins, and her mom has been there to support her every step of the way.

As the days turned into weeks and the weeks into months, the children still were not speaking. Moreover, they seemed to grow more and more apathetic. King Frederick made sure they received good nourishment and basic care from the staff, but nevertheless the children exhibited none of the normal curiosity and interaction most children demonstrate. Frederick persisted, however, insisting that there be no physical or verbal contact between any adult and any child.

A child needs touching. A child needs contact. Even before conception a parent should listen for the song of her child. And prenatal bonding contributes to the development of the unborn child. There have been several pioneering studies, especially the *firstart* program in Valencia, Venezuela, that demonstrate quite conclusively the positive effect of prenatal stimulation on the development of a child. Beyond scientific study, however, every mother knows instinctively the importance of talking, singing, and meditating with her unborn child. And when Dad as well is involved in prenatal massage and conversations, the family unit is bonding even before the beautiful child has poked his head out of the womb.

It is so important to know that parenting begins before you even see your child! When a child is born, he needs to continue this attachment to his mother as much as his mother needs to continue the bonding with her child. The process is a two-way street, important for the health of both mother and child. After all, that child has spent nine months in total intimacy with his mom. He should not suddenly be separated from his life support system. In fact, studies show that when a mother and child make eye contact immediately after delivery, there is a brain linkup between the mother's and the baby's right brains. This link encourages the child's development.

In Bali, a tradition exists that when a child is born, he is not allowed to touch the earth for nine months. The belief is that the transition from heaven to earth should be gradual, not sudden. In families that follow this tradition, the child is passed from mother to father to grandparent to uncle and aunt. It quite literally takes a village to raise a child in Bali.

Skeptics would have you believe that a child constantly held will grow up weak and insecure. For generations, mothers have been told to let their children cry themselves to sleep, don't pick them up or give them too much affection. Nonsense. A child who gets all his needs met when he is a child grows into a more secure teenager and adult, whereas a child who suffers from *attachment disorder,* a condition stemming from lack of bonding early in life, will tend to grow up with infantile personality dysfunction. The extreme version of this problem is with adopted children, especially in the countries of eastern Europe, where several hundred thousand orphans are institutionalized in extremely primitive psychological conditions. These orphans develop serious disabilities and special needs that go largely untreated. On the other hand, the children in Bali, graced by tender holding since the day of their birth, grow into happy, stable, strong, and productive members of their community.

In the USA and other countries, we have another emerging problem. Due to economic necessity as well as the feminist movement, more and more mothers are leaving their children at an earlier age. As two parents must work to support a household, a subculture of baby-sitters, daycare workers, and alternative child care has emerged. While conditions are often excellent in such situations, there is no perfect substitute for the genuine love and presence of a mother. We are suffering as a society when we let go of the family breakfast and dinner. A time for gathering, sharing, and supporting has gradually eroded into a time for everyone to be on their own.

Although we can raise our awareness and improve this situation, or wrongdoing, we should not be motivated by feelings of guilt or blame. But we should be clear that we are raising a generation of fairly unattached children. Some of them can seem quite independent at an early age, well-behaved, golden on the outside but steel inside. They might do fine in front of a computer, a Game Boy, or a PlayStation, but in terms of interactive relationships with other humans, they might be lagging in their social skills. Deep down inside, they are angry about not being touched, afraid of being touched, and perhaps vindictive. There are no studies, but it would not surprise me in the least to discover that the "killer children" of Columbine High School suffered from some *attachment disorder*. At the very least, we know that these children suffered from low self-esteem, peer pressure, feeling excluded, not belonging, and deeply rooted rejection.

An experiment with cows, reported by Dr. Michel Odente at an Association for Pre- and Perinatal Psychology and Health (APPPAH) Congress in San Francisco in December 1999, is illuminating. Dr. Odente, who is conducting a study on the consequences of anesthesia on civilization, spoke of cows that were anesthetized during labor. They were therefore unable to bond with their babies, which consequently could not attach to or feed from them after birth. The result was that the baby cows became angrier and angrier, eventually exhibiting severe antisocial behavior.

Hold your children! From the time of their birth and throughout their lives, they need touching, affection, and physical reassuring. We all do. The value of the chemistry that occurs between a parent and a child when there is tender touching cannot be overestimated. I believe it stimulates a healthy heart, a healthy brain, and a healthy immune system. If you feel uneasy about such touching because you did not receive it from your parents, then do the work of completing the past with them, thus liberating yourself to love your children in healthier ways.

About a hundred years ago, at the turn of another century, orphanages were incredibly terrible places, even here in the USA. Yes, there was malnutrition, but this was not the worst problem. Far more serious was that children were growing up without appropriate adult touching. The death rate in some of these orphanages approached 90 percent.

When was the last time you hugged your child?

By the time the children were one year old, it was clear that Frederick the Great's experiment in creating a universal language was a complete failure. All one hundred children had died. None of them had ever been touched!

Index

A

Abuse, 20, 26, 110–11, 147
Acknowledgment. *See* Recognition
Addiction
  to alcohol and drugs, 31
  to healing, 31–32, 40
  root of, 97
Affirmations, 33, 61, 62
Aggression, 129
Alcoholics Anonymous, 31
Apologies, 8, 111–12
Attachment disorder, 150–51
Auras, 108

B

Beauty, 67–68
Birth
  learning before, 5–6, 149–50
  trauma of, 29, 112
Black Madonna, 95
Body image, 67–68
Buddha, 130

C

Caretaking, 55
Charity, 127–28
Children. *See also* Family
  apologizing to, 111
  attachment disorder, 150–51
  education of, 24–25

  holding, 143–51
  learning before birth, 5–6,
    149–50
  love and, 81
  mistakes made by, 106–7, 148
  parents' support of, 49–50
  praising and rewarding, 6–7, 65,
    75
  respect and, 19–20, 146
  self-esteem of, 4–7, 65, 146–47
  setting boundaries for, 66, 148
  unwanted, 5–6, 61, 64, 144
Closure, 37
Codependency, 55, 109
Compassion
  humility and, 127
  for oneself, 5
  for the world, 115
Competition, 128–29
A Course in Miracles, 33, 35, 129

D

Denial, 34
Diversity, celebrating, 18
Dyadic dance, 18–19

E

Education, 24–25
Egotism, spiritual, 123
Einstein, Albert, 91, 130, 131